SKOKIE PUBLIC LIBRARY

SO-ARH-538

JAN   2013

Praise for *Likeable Business*

"From transparency to authenticity to the impact of sharing one's values via story telling—Dave Kerpen's blueprints on how to run a business move from 'Likeable' to essential. Ben & Jerry's was founded on these values in 1978 and has practiced them through the company's phenomenal growth to this very day. With communication at digital speeds in today's corporate world, it's no longer a choice to be responsible. Consumers choose to support businesses who practice values-led business. The opportunities when running your business in a responsible manner allow great freedom within your organization and externally with the ever-growing conscious consumer world around us."

—Jostein Solheim, CEO of Ben & Jerry's

"Dave provides a blueprint that allows entrepreneurs everywhere to build a successful, likeable business in this era of social media."

—Scott Gerber, founder of Young Entrepreneurs Council

"A masterful storyteller, Dave Kerpen takes you on a journey into the wonderful new world of tomorrow. It's a place where customers love you and ensure your business success. This is no wishful utopia. It's a reality within reach if you follow the principles of *Likeable Business*."

—Michael Stelzner, CEO of Social Media Examiner
and author of *Launch: How to Quickly Propel
Your Business Beyond the Competition*

"Social media teaches businesses how to be nicer to people—and be happier while doing it. This book will teach you how to make that change for your entire business—and make more money because you're doing it."

—Andy Sernovitz, *New York Times* bestselling
author of *Word of Mouth Marketing:
How Smart Companies Get People Talking*

"Likeability matters. It opens doors and minds and makes everything easier. But, how do you 'build' a likeable business? In *Likeable Business*, Kerpen shares a validated step-by-step path to likeability. A great read for entrepreneurs and executives alike!"

—Jonathan Fields, author of *Uncertainty*
and founder of Good Life Project™

"It's simple; when people understand who you are and where you come from, they're more likely to rally around your cause. Every company has its own unique history, one that's worth sharing. At 1-800-GOT-JUNK? we're passionate about sharing where we came from and where we're headed not only with our customers and the public but within our own teams."

—Brian Scudamore, founder and CEO of 1-800-GOT-JUNK?

likeable
business

likeable
business

Why Today's **CONSUMERS DEMAND MORE**
and How **LEADERS CAN DELIVER**

DAVE KERPEN

with

Theresa Braun and Valerie Pritchard

Mc
Graw
Hill

New York   Chicago   San Francisco   Lisbon   London   Madrid   Mexico City
Milan   New Delhi   San Juan   Seoul   Singapore   Sydney   Toronto

SKOKIE PUBLIC LIBRARY

The **McGraw·Hill** Companies

Copyright © 2013 by Dave Kerpen. All rights reserved. Printed in the United States of America. Except as permitted under the United States Copyright Act of 1976, no part of this publication may be reproduced or distributed in any form or by any means, or stored in a database or retrieval system, without the prior written permission of the publisher.

1 2 3 4 5 6 7 8 9 10   FGR/FGR   1 8 7 6 5 4 3 2

ISBN 978-0-07-180047-1 (paperback)
MHID 0-07-180047-6

ISBN 978-0-07-181373-0 (hardcover)
MHID 0-07-181373-X

e-ISBN 978-0-07-180048-8
e-MHID 0-07-180048-4

While the author and publisher have done their best to ensure that the screen shots presented in this book are current at the time of printing, the reader must be aware that due to the ever-evolving technology of the medium, it is impossible to guarantee the accuracy of every single screen shot once the book has been published.

Library of Congress Cataloging-in-Publication Data
Kerpen, Dave.
  Likeable business : why today's consumers demand more and how leaders can deliver / by Dave Kerpen.
      p. cm.
  ISBN 978-0-07-180047-1 (alk. paper) — ISBN 0-07-180047-6 (alk. paper)
  1. Management—Social aspects.   2. Customer relations.   3. Social responsibility of business.   I. Title.
  HD31.K4585   2013
  658.8'12—dc23

                                                                    2012032549

McGraw-Hill books are available at special quantity discounts to use as premiums and sales promotions or for use in corporate training programs. To contact a representative, please e-mail us at bulksales@mcgraw-hill.com.

This book is printed on acid-free paper.

STOCKPORT LIBRARY

Thank you
so much for purchasing
the hardcover edition of
Likeable Business!

As a special bonus just for you,
please visit
http://bit.ly/LikeableBusinessBonus
to download 3 free ebook singles:

- An Introductory Guide to Content Strategy

- The Ultimate Guide to Mastering ROI for Your Business

- Likeable Business Extended: Articles and Ideas

This book is dedicated to the most likeable person I know, Carrie. You are an inspiring leader, an amazing mom, a loving wife, and a truly likeable—no, loveable—woman. #InItTogether

Contents

ACKNOWLEDGMENTS FROM DAVE

Those of you who know me (and know the giant social media universe) know that there are literally thousands of people I'd like to thank here. But since that wouldn't make for very good reading material, I'll summarize by key categories. If your name isn't listed, but you're among my extended group of friends, family, colleagues, and supporters, please know how appreciative I am of you and your impact on my life.

My Likeable Coauthors

After everything you've done for this book, Theresa and Valerie, it's hard for me to believe I wrote a book on my own before this one. Thank you, Val, for your excellent research and interviews. You have a bright future ahead of you. Thank you, Theresa, for your tireless work on and dedication to this book and for your uncanny ability to capture my voice and vision. You are an excellent writer, and I can't wait to read your next work.

My Likeable Publishing Family

Thanks to the all the editors and staff at McGraw-Hill Professional who worked on the book and showed me there is still room for traditional publishers today. Thanks especially to Stephanie Frerich, my acquisitions editor, who gave us the leeway to write the book we believed in. Thanks to my agent, Celeste Fine at Sterling Lord, a likeable agent who continues to help me navigate the crazy changing waters of publishing.

My Likeable Work Family

I am so incredibly fortunate to be surrounded by an amazing team at my company, Likeable Media. Thanks to all of you for your support: Mallorie Rosenbluth, Jenna Lebel, Megan McMahon, Michele Weisman, Amy Kattan, Lauren Sleeper, Ike Brooker, Allie Herzog, Cara Friedman, Dean Opriasa, Dhara Naik, Andi Barton, Brian Murray, Amanda Diantonio, Gaby Piazza, Carrie Tylawsky, Ricky Demaio, Marissa Breton, Tim Bosch, Frank Emanuele, Katie Kearsey, Shari Donk, Ramon Thompson, Rodney Hazard, Louie Cale, Nicole Mastrangelo, Sam Sudakoff, Ben Lieblich, and all our Buzz Builders and part-timers. Also, thanks to our incredible Likeable Advisory Board: Christian McMahan, Robb High, Peg Jackson, Chris McCann, Ed Zuckerberg, Julie Fenster, Craig Gibson, Michael Lasky, Jeffrey Hayzlett, Mark Roberge, and Nihal Mehta. Finally, thanks to Jonas Ortega and the team at Likeable Tu and Can Ozinci and the team at Likeable Istanbul. You—and the whole Likeable team—RULE!

My Likeable EO Family

Thanks to my Forum—Andy Cohen, Ben Rosner, Ce Ce Chin, Vinnie Cannariato, Kevin Gilbert, Andrew Thornton, Jennifer Busch, and Jeff Bernstein. Thanks to my fellow board members, especially Richard Humphrey and Shep Sepaniak. Thanks to Cary Chessick, a special YPO friend, and the rest of my friends from Entrepreneurs Organization who have changed my life in so many ways.

My Likeable Online Family

There are dozens of social media and business thought leaders who have influenced me, taught me, shared with me, and inspired me. Some I'm close friends with, others I've never met, but all of you on this list (and beyond) have had a profound impact on my view of the world. (They should all be followed on Twitter too!) So thanks to Seth Godin, Neil Glassman, Mari Smith, John Bell, Jason Keath, Peter Shankman, Chris Brogan, Scott Stratten, Jay Baer, Guy Kawasaki, Clara Shih, David Kirkpatrick, Scott Monty, Erik Qualman, Brian Solis, Aaron Lee, Tony Hsieh, Josh Bernoff, Nick O'Neill, Justin Smith, Amber Naslund, Liz Strauss, Sarah Evans, Todd Defren, Charlene Li, David Berkowitz, Geno Church, Jeff Pulver, Leslie Bradshaw, Jesse Thomas, John Jantsch, David Meerman Scott, Rohit Bhargava, Brian Carter, Shiv Singh, Ashton Kutcher, Greg Verdino, Bonin Bough, Andy Sernovitz, Pete Blackshaw, BL Ochman, Mike Maddock, Jim Collins, Barbara Corcoran, Mark Cuban. Brian Moran, John Warrillow, Frank Eliason, and Verne Harnish. Thank you all, and keep up the amazing work.

My Loveable Family

Okay, I'm counting close friends here too. Thanks to my World Tour friends, Steve Evangelista, Kevin Annanab, Tad Bruneau, Danny Morgenbesser, and Andy Kaufmann, for allowing me to take a break and have some fun during the crazy writing process. Thanks to my Aunt Lisa and Uncle Mark for being a steady, positive family and business influence; my Da for her unconditional love and support; my brother Phil and his wife, Joanna; my brother Danny and his wife, Erin; and my brother-in-law Dan. Thanks to my mom, Rayni Joan, and my dad, Peter Kerpen.

Last, but most important, thanks to my women at home. To my girls, Charlotte and Kate, thanks for continually impressing me with your smarts, talents, and ability to care so much about the world around you. I am so proud of you both and love you so much. To Carrie, my partner in marriage, business, parenthood, and life, for you I am most thankful. You continue to believe in me even when I don't believe in myself. You are my friend, my lover, my business partner, and my coach. I love you and look forward to continuing to be #inittogether with you.

Thanks to all the amazing, likeable people who helped *Likeable Business* get to your hands.

ACKNOWLEDGMENTS FROM THERESA

First and foremost, I would like to thank Dave Kerpen for trusting me and giving me a shot—with this book and at Likeable as a whole. Your faith in my ability means the world to me.

Valerie Pritchard, thank you for your hard work, reliability, and shared fro yo cravings. There's no way I could have tackled this project without you.

Carrie Kerpen, I am so grateful for your guidance and support. Thanks for always being available to chat (and reminding me when it's past my bedtime).

Members of the #letsgo Spring and Summer 2012 teams (Pavel Konoplenko, Kathy Conway, Melanie Niklas, Stephany Xu, Sarah Weg, Jon Kordi-Hubbard, Daria Preston, Janice Hernandez, Meghan Breneman, Joi Moore, Laura Perez, and Ali Lifton), thank you for tracking down facts, pictures, and some of my sanity.

My two favorite photographers, DJ Switz and Cliff Sebastian, thank you for helping out in a pinch.

To the entire Likeable staff: thank you for teaching me what it means to truly be likeable.

Much thanks also to family and friends, especially:

My parents, John and Mary Braun, and my sisters, Sarah and Meghan Braun, for being my cheerleaders and never failing to quote important words of family wisdom

Courtney and Joe Peters and their children Burke and Bridget, for always giving me a place to call home—and for filling that home with love, silliness, and pinot noir

My New York saviors, the Doherty and Shaw families, for taking in a stray

Kelsey Healey, for being the wisest, wittiest writer I know (not to mention the best friend)

Annie McAndrews and Alfredo Gil, for never failing to be there when it matters most (nor failing to make me giggle when it's needed most)

Julia May, for inspiring, advising, and funkifying
Will Abeles, for just plain putting up with me during "Book
  Mode"

And to anyone who's ever helped me face a fear, been my roommate, or complimented my outfit: I sincerely thank you.

ACKNOWLEDGMENTS FROM VAL

First, I'd like to thank Dave for trusting me with the daunting task that was writing this book, and Theresa for being the "glue" and pulling this thing together. It wasn't easy, but I'm proud of what we've accomplished.

Second, I want to thank my family as a group for being such a great support system. Thank you all for reading my blog posts, laughing at my dumb jokes, posting embarrassing pictures of me from middle school on the Internet, and offering support when I need it most. A more specific thank you goes to my sisters for achieving great things and igniting the ever-present youngest-sibling desire to beat you at everything. Thank you to my parents for your constant advice, encouragement, and weirdness. And of course, thank you to my brilliant and hilarious grandmother, whose stories and successful career as a journalist inspired me to pick up the pen in the first place.

Third, I want to thank my friends. Martine and Gabrielle, thank you for being the most hilarious roommates a person could ask for. Lauren and Brant (and Eleanor, I suppose), thank you for being such a great support system, especially from a distance. I can't wait to be neighbors again! Michael, thank you for giving me the best advice out of anyone I know on all things career or book related. In no particular order, I'd like to thank Rachel, Monica, Greg, Cindy, Simone, Davod, Avi, Shane, and Aimee for being generally amazing not just during the book process, but for all the time I've known them.

Finally, I want to thank my teachers and professors who helped me become the writer and person I am today. There are too many to list here, but know I will always have an immense respect and appreciation for all of you.

If there is anyone who I have neglected to mention, rest assured that I certainly do appreciate all of your help, guidance, and support.

Don't worry. It's just a cocktail party.

As I stood over my father's hospital bed, I felt a profound sense of hopelessness, anger, and frustration. For two weeks I had witnessed the rapid deterioration of my dad's health at Beth Israel Hospital in New York, from the time he entered until now. My dad had gone into the hospital with breathing issues, had been diagnosed with a pulmonary embolism, and had been given a good prognosis for quick recovery. But instead, as I looked at him, he could barely speak, had no idea what was happening around him, and was a shell of himself, slipping in and out of consciousness.

That alone would have been terrifying and frustrating—but that wasn't what I was so angry about. I was angry because I had visited my dad twice without a doctor seeing me, and I'd left no fewer than 13 telephone messages for his doctor, none of which had been responded to. I had told nurses upon my visit that something was very wrong, and they looked at me like I was crazy. Something was wrong, all right: how my dad and I were being treated by this hospital.

Desperate for a response, I turned to a public social media channel for help and posted on the hospital's Facebook page. Within minutes, a Patient Relations representative responded and told me how to get in touch with her. I spoke with her, and soon after, I spoke with the doctor. The doctor finally took a closer look at my dad, realized he had had a negative reaction to the medications he had been on while in the hospital, and quickly moved him to intensive care, where he was treated and his life was saved.

I am so thankful that things turned out as they did. But why did it have to come to a crisis point? Why did I have to hold Beth

Israel accountable on Facebook in order to get a response from my father's doctor?

My first book was *Likeable Social Media: How to Delight Your Customers, Create an Irresistible Brand, and Be Generally Amazing on Facebook (and Other Social Networks)*. It featured chapters on using social media to listen, be responsive, and share and inspire stories. As I wrote the book and gave speeches on the subject, I realized how many of those principles don't apply only to social media but to business in general. It isn't just important to listen to your customers on Twitter; it's important to listen to your customers everywhere. It isn't just important to be responsive to customers on Facebook; it's important to be responsive to customers everywhere. It isn't just important to be able to tell a great story on the social web; it's important to tell a great story everywhere, whether you're socializing at a cocktail party, meeting in the boardroom, or delivering a big sales pitch.

In order to be successful in today's society, businesspeople must be obsessed with their customers and prospects, and always doing right by them. This book will take the principles of *Likeable Social Media* and apply them to business in general—how to become a likeable leader of a likeable business, one worth talking about in a positive way.

Unfortunately, there are still far more stories of unlikeable businesses than likeable ones. In June 2006, Brian Finkelstein was frustrated about the extremely poor customer service he had received from his cable television company, Comcast. After missed appointments and broken routers, his opportunity for revenge came when a Comcast technician actually fell asleep on the couch after being put on hold for so long by his own company. Finkelstein shot a quick video and uploaded it to the Internet. Over 2 million people have now seen the video, "A Comcast Technician Sleeping on My Couch," surely negatively affecting Comcast's reputation and brand.

The good news is, Comcast responded. Frank Eliason, then the customer service manager, started a program called "Comcast Cares" in 2007, and Comcast thus became an early example of a business proactively using Twitter to resolve customer service issues and strengthen relationships with customers.[1]

On July 6, 2009, aspiring singer Dave Carroll uploaded a video onto YouTube he called "United Breaks Guitars." The video tells the story of a United Airlines flight during which Carroll's guitar was broken. Far worse than breaking his guitar, thought Carroll, was United's refusal to pay for it and the company's rudeness to him following his flight. Carroll didn't call the media—he just made a little video and uploaded it to the world's largest online video community. United didn't respond to the video, but the public did. In just three years, over 12 million people have viewed Carroll's video, potentially damaging United's reputation—and stock price.

At the same time, rival airline JetBlue has established itself as a leader in online and offline responsiveness, with industry-leading Twitter account @jetblue and shorter-than-average phone wait times.[2] While most other U.S. airlines have struggled in financial performance, JetBlue has grown 80 percent over the past five years.[3]

Have you ever had a bad experience with a hospital? How about a cable television company? Or an airline? Or a local business? Or a rude salesperson or office manager? For many years, companies large and small have struggled with how they treat their customers and prospects. But the times have changed. It used to be that a customer shared a bad experience with a company privately, through a comment card. Now it's shared publicly on Facebook, Twitter, or YouTube. It used to be that a customer shared a bad experience with several friends. Now it's shared with several hundred. Or several thousand. Or several million. And companies have no choice but to listen.

Twenty-five years ago, mediocre companies could spend lots of money on television ads or cold calls and generate lots of sales. Poor customer service, poor follow-up, or bad products didn't matter. Today, everything matters. Today, being likeable matters.

THE ROLE OF SOCIAL MEDIA IN TODAY'S SOCIETY

When I was a child, I remember a family meal at a local diner that led to three of us getting food poisoning. My mom called the restaurant and complained, threatening to call the local media and have the restaurant written up in our local newspaper. Twenty-five years later, that newspaper no longer exists. In fact, the entire face of media has changed. I now have more Twitter followers than the circulation of many small-town newspapers, at least those that are still around.

What happened? While newspapers were shrinking and folding, the social web was born. Facebook went from nothing to a billion users worldwide in nine years. Twitter went from nothing to 500 million users in seven years. People went from getting information from linear media and sharing it with a few friends to getting information from social media and then resharing it with many friends.

It's important to note that while I may have lots of connections via social media, and while you may have lots of connections via social media, and while online influence matters to a certain extent, it's the medium that's more important than the individual when it comes to sharing messages. You may not know the name "Janis Krums," but you have probably seen his photograph of a plane crashing into the Hudson River in New York City (see Figure I.1).

FIGURE I.1 **Janis Krums had just 170 followers when he tweeted this picture, soon seen around the world.**
Source: Janis Krums

Many millions of people have seen this picture, which Krums tweeted. Yet Krums had only 170 followers on Twitter the day he shared the picture. The picture resonated extremely well with a few people, who shared it with others, who in turn shared it again until it was also shared through linear media such as television—and within a few hours, it spread and spread and spread. Text, pictures, and videos such as "United Breaks Guitars" are created and shared by millions of people each day in the new social web. Today, you don't need to call up the local media when you have something to say—you *are* the local media.

WHAT THIS ALL MEANS: OBSESSION WITH THE CUSTOMER

In a hyperconnected, social media–driven society, businesses can no longer afford to be mediocre. Businesses large and small must be obsessed with their customers, making and keeping them happy. If it seems scary that one disgruntled customer could negatively impact your business, it is scary. But obsession with your customers cannot only stave off negative results; it can lead to extremely positive results as well. The people who can share negative stories through social media can also share positive ones. In the same way that stories of customer service failures can spread quickly, so can stories of going above and beyond to delight your customers.

BUT YOUR CUSTOMERS CAN'T BE YOUR ONLY OBSESSION

At your organization, the people you interact with as much as—if not more than—your customers are your colleagues and employees. Being likeable isn't just about your customers. After all, if the people at your company aren't passionate about what they do, don't work well together as a team, don't listen to one another, and don't enjoy a strong company culture, how can they possibly create amazing experiences for your customers? In every chapter, we'll explore not only what it means to be likeable externally, but what it means to be likeable internally, within your organization. It really is all about the people.

WHO THIS BOOK IS FOR (AND NOT FOR)

This book is for anyone who wants to become a more likeable leader. This book is for marketers and executives at small, medium, and large companies. Especially at large companies, where change is more difficult, it's going to take a lot of internal brand ambassadors—or likeable leaders—to effect real change. Companies must rethink and reorganize not only the way they do business around their customers, but the way they empower their people to become likeable leaders.

This book is also for small-business owners and entrepreneurs with new ideas. This book is for lawyers, doctors, dentists, accountants, and consultants who are progressive thinkers and are ready to change the way they conduct business. This book is for salespeople, independent and otherwise, whose livelihoods rely on building their own minibusiness within a business.

This book is for leaders in government and at nonprofit organizations, who should have an easier time selling ideas to their constituents but who often struggle with many of the same challenges of today's businesses. This book is for students and teachers of business and for students of our new social media–driven society and the problems and opportunities the new media creates for business.

This book is *not* for data junkies who want to sift through mounds of research. I will share lots of stories to illustrate my points; and for some, that's a lot of fun, but for data junkies, something will be missing. This book is not for those who want the latest tools to optimize their presence online—no book can stay up to date on this subject, and so I suggest you turn to blogs.

This book is for everyone who is a customer, who agrees that organizations need to be more likeable and wants to be part of the solution, online and offline.

What makes a social media entrepreneur capable of writing a business book? You'll read more of my story later. But Likeable Media, the company started in 2007, has benefited from triple-digit revenue growth for four consecutive years. We've been fortunate enough to be on *Inc. Magazine*'s Inc. 500 list of the fastest growing private companies in the United States for both 2011 and 2012. More important, our team lives and breathes five core values: passion, drive, transparency, thought leadership, and adaptability. Three of these are explored a lot further in the book, but I'd like to think we have in our team most of the 11 qualities of a likeable business.

Our story is just one of many, though. We've interviewed dozens of successful companies, large and small, for this book, asking each what qualities helped it succeed as a company. We've asked CEOs what likeable qualities they have and which ones really resonate with them. We've talked to leaders and managers at a wide variety of organizations of all sizes, looking for stories and case studies that bring to light the concepts of a likeable business. And we've documented companies whose unlikeable practices have led to disaster.

THE 11 PRINCIPLES OF LIKEABLE BUSINESS

We will explore 11 principles of likeable business that together make for more likeable leaders and better, more customer-centric organizations (see Figure I.2).

1. **Listening.** Listening is the foundation of any good business. Great leaders listen to what their customers and prospects want and need, and they listen to the challenges those customers face. They listen to colleagues and are open to new ideas. They listen to shareholders, investors, and competitors.
2. **Storytelling.** After listening, leaders need to tell great stories in order to sell their products, but, more important, in order to sell their ideas. Storytelling is what captivates people and drives them to take action. A likeable leader has a strong vision and purpose and always has stories to sell that vision.

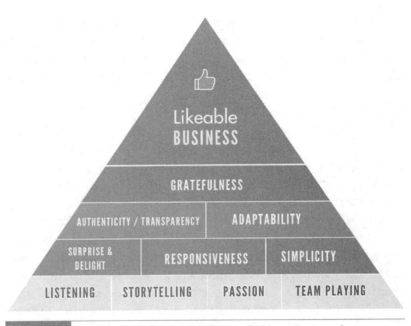

FIGURE I.2 **The Likeable Pyramid shows the foundations for a likeable business.**
Source: Ramon Thompson

3. **Authenticity.** Great leaders are who they say they are, and they have integrity beyond compare. Vulnerability and humility are hallmarks of the authentic leader and create a positive, attractive energy. Customers, employees, and media all want to help an authentic person to succeed. There used to be a divide between one's public self and private self, but the social Internet has blurred that line. Likeable leaders are transparent about who they are online, merging their personal and professional life together.

4. **Transparency.** There is nowhere to hide anymore, and businesspeople who attempt to keep secrets will eventually be exposed. Openness and honesty lead to happier staff and customers—and a happier you.

5. **Team Playing.** No matter how small your organization, you interact with others every day. Letting others shine, encouraging innovative ideas, and following other rules for working in teams will help you become a more likeable leader. You'll

need a culture of success within your organization, one that includes out-of-the-box thinking.

6. **Responsiveness.** Today's leaders are responsive to their customers, staff, investors, and prospects. Every stakeholder is a potential viral sparkplug, for better or for worse, and the winning leader is one who recognizes this and insists upon a culture of responsiveness. Responding shows you care and gives your customers and employees a say, allowing them to make a positive impact on your company.

7. **Adaptability.** There has never been a faster-changing marketplace than the one we live in today. Leaders must be flexible in managing changing opportunities and challenges and nimble enough to pivot at the right moment. Stubbornness is no longer desirable. Instead, humility and the willingness to adapt mark a great leader.

8. **Passion.** Those who love what they do don't have to work a day in their lives. People who are able to bring passion to their business have a remarkable advantage, as that passion is contagious to customers and colleagues alike. Finding and increasing your passion will absolutely affect your bottom line.

9. **Surprise and Delight.** Most people like surprises in their day-to-day lives. Likeable leaders underpromise and overdeliver, assuring that customers and staff are surprised in a positive way. We'll explore a plethora of ways to surprise without spending extra money. We all like to be delighted, and surprise and delight create incredible word-of-mouth marketing opportunities.

10. **Simplicity.** The world is more complex than ever before, and yet what customers often respond to best is simplicity—in design, form, and function. Taking complex projects, challenges, and ideas and distilling them to their simplest components allows customers, staff, and other stakeholders to better understand and buy into your vision. We humans all crave simplicity, and so the likeable leader must be focused and deliver simplicity.

11. **Gratefulness.** Finally, likeable leaders are ever grateful for the people who contribute to their opportunities and success. Being appreciative and saying thank you to mentors,

customers, colleagues, and other stakeholders keeps leaders humble, appreciated, and well received. It also makes you feel great, and karma is often returned to the bottom line.

We'll also explore each principle's implications for the increasingly social business. In other words, how does each principle apply to the use of social media both internally and externally in order to build a likeable business? Again, this isn't a social media book per se, but the reality is that all the principles of a likeable business apply to a social business as well. And if your organization is going to thrive in today's world, you'll have to embrace "social," not as a way to put up Facebook pages and Twitter accounts and "do marketing," but as a way to transform your business from the inside out.

Obviously, not all leaders possess all 11 of these qualities, but most of the greatest leaders of large and small organizations exemplify at least some of them. The stories we'll explore demonstrate how powerful these qualities are in building a likeable business—and a more profitable one.

If the CEO of a large company is responsive, adaptable, and passionate, does that guarantee that a customer won't have an experience like those in "United Breaks Guitars" or "A Comcast Technician Sleeping on My Couch"? Of course not. But these qualities in leaders establish the all-important culture of an organization, which in turn affects the experience of customers. Leaders in any organization set the tone for the people who work for them, who eventually set the tone for the products and services and customers' experiences. And in today's world, every customer's experience matters more than ever before.

THE ROLE OF THE CONSUMER IN CREATING A MORE LIKEABLE WORLD

In January, I took my family on the most amazing vacation of my life, to the Beaches Resort in Turks and Caicos. We were there for only four days, but our time was jam-packed with fun activities, the weather and beach were gorgeous, and the staff at

Beaches was nothing short of perfect. The Sesame Street character integration was fantastic, as my kids were not only able to take photos with Big Bird, Elmo, and Zoe, but able to hang out with them, play games, and have a dance party. To top it all off, on our last night there, Zoe came to our hotel room and tucked in my girls, reading them a story and creating a memory that will surely last a lifetime for all of us (see Figure I.3).

I've not just told that story here—I've told it to thousands of people on Facebook, Twitter, Instagram, and Google+.

When I have issues with companies or with customer service reps or salespeople, I share those issues with the world through social media. I hold companies to high standards of products and service, and when those standards aren't met, I share. Shouldn't we all? But I also share stories of likeable businesses, leaders, and experiences. I want the world to know about the good businesspeople and organizations out there, who listen to their customers, respond to changing needs, and are passionate and grateful.

It's likely that you're a businessperson, salesperson, or leader in your organization. But most certainly you're a consumer as

FIGURE I.3   **Thanks to social media, now thousands of people know about this likeable experience.**
Source: Dave Kerpen

well. As consumers, we all have the opportunity—and I would argue the responsibility—to share the good *and* bad experiences we have.

You have the opportunity to hold unlikeable businesses and leaders accountable through social networks, and businesses have the opportunity to receive direct and immediate feedback from their consumers. When Netflix changed its policy in September 2011 and planned to launch Qwikster, the world reacted, and Netflix immediately changed course. The social web even allowed protesters to unite and overthrow unlikeable leaders in Egypt (Hosni Mubarak) and Libya (Muammar Gaddafi) in 2011.

With that opportunity comes the responsibility for consumers to share good stories about the likeable leaders and companies who make our lives better, put smiles on our faces, and provide simple products and services that add value. As you read the stories and principles of likeable business that I'll share, I challenge you to think about not only how you can change your organization, but how you as a consumer can recognize other likeable businesses—and in turn share your own stories.

LET'S GET LIKEABLE!

One of the key leadership traits we'll explore is responsiveness. It's one of my core values, and I continue to respond to any and all tweets and Facebook messages that come my way each day. As you read, please know that I always remain open to feedback, questions, thoughts, and ideas. Connect with me and ask questions as you go, on Twitter (Twitter.com/DaveKerpen) and Facebook (FB.com/LikeableBook). Now let's get likeable.

CHAPTER 1

Listening

One Mouth, Two Ears, Many Opportunities

When people talk, listen completely. Most people never listen.

—Ernest Hemingway

I finally decided to take my own advice and shut up and listen. For five years I'd been leading a company in social media marketing, preaching about the value of listening using social media. I had written *Likeable Social Media,* which featured "Listen First and Never Stop Listening" as the title of Chapter 1. I had spoken to thousands of people at live events about the virtues of listening to customers and colleagues. Yet I suffered from the same syndrome as many leaders: I have a lot of ideas, and I liked to share them. That meant talking, which, unfortunately, by definition, meant not listening. I wanted to better understand how my team could work without me. I wanted to begin practicing what I preached. So I shut up and conducted an hour-long management team meeting without saying a word.

At first, people were shocked. They weren't sure what to say. They asked me a few questions, to which I just shook my head to silently say, "I'm just listening today. Carry on." What followed was amazing: Managers rose to the challenge and led without me. People shared their own ideas—some of which I didn't like, but others I absolutely loved. A few people remained silent, which was okay, but people who probably wouldn't have spoken in the meeting spoke, and others spoke more—they had the time to, because I wasn't talking. My listening was a gift in that it gave others the chance to be heard. Of course, it was also invaluable to me, as I gained insight into people's thinking and problem-solving skills, ideas and wishes, even strengths and weaknesses. All from one hour of shutting up and listening.

Practice makes perfect, and months later, I now have a lot of practice listening, but I'm still far from perfect. I'll always be a bit of a crazy-idea-guy entrepreneur, and I think I may always struggle with the listening-versus-talking challenge. But the more I listen, the more I learn.

WHAT IS LISTENING, IN A BUSINESS SENSE?

Merriam-Webster defines listening as "hearing something with thoughtful attention: giving consideration." Listening is clearly more than just hearing. It is the act of consciously paying attention to someone else, with an attempt to understand, to consider. It is the process of thinking about what is important to someone else rather than what may be important to you. It is the act, at any given moment, of caring more about what someone else has to say than anything else in the world. Listening is hard—a lot harder than you might think. There is also ample evidence that listening is more difficult for men than for women.[1] Think about how challenging it is for some of us to shut up and listen while dating and in relationships. So half of us are off to a challenging start.

WHY IS LISTENING SO DIFFICULT FOR LEADERS, YET SO IMPORTANT?

Leaders, businesspeople, and entrepreneurs are full of ideas. Many of you have ideas all day long every day about how to make the world a better place, make money, and solve problems. The very nature of active listening requires us to put aside our ideas completely, if only for a moment, in order to focus on what someone else has to say.

As difficult as that can be, it's through listening to customers, prospective customers, colleagues, employees, and others that we can better understand what their needs and motivations are—and ultimately make our ideas better and more executable. It's leaders like you who need to learn to listen better, even more so than the world's followers.

When I first started out, as a salesperson for Radio Disney at the age of 22, I was young and foolish (well, even younger and more foolish than I am today). I thought that I had a great product to sell and that people would love to listen to me talk about it. I thought that I could be charming and persuasive and convince decision makers why it made sense to use my product to solve their marketing problems.

I thought wrong. I was failing miserably, despite what I considered my charm and persuasion. A few weeks into the job, my mentor, Peggy Iafrate, said to me, "How well are you listening to what your prospects have to say? How many questions are you asking them to better understand them? How are you showing them that you care about them more than you care about selling to them?"

I hadn't been doing a very good job of listening. In fact, by my very nature, I'm one of the people I described above: full of thoughts, running a mile a minute, an impatient New York male who always has something to say and never slows down. So it took some real dedication and practice to listen to what Peggy told me about listening and heed her advice.

I began asking my prospects more questions. Listening to their problems, listening to their interests, listening to their every word became my obsession. I thought very little about how to sell them on advertising with Radio Disney and instead focused on listening attentively to everything they had to say so that I could better understand them as people and better understand their organizational needs and challenges. Once I understood them, I could do a much better job of delivering what they wanted and needed, both in the product I was selling and in the way I sold it.

Things quickly started to fall into place once I started listening. Within six months, I was the number one local salesperson in the country, and a year later Peggy awarded me the Mickey Award for sales success. All for shutting up and listening.

NETFLIX SCREWS UP, BUT LISTENS

Netflix executives made a series of very unpopular decisions during the summer of 2011. They began with a price hike for all their services, and then they announced that Netflix services would be splitting in two: DVD rentals and streaming services would each get their own account information, billing information, passwords, and queues. To top it off, the DVD mailing service would be featured on a new site call Qwikster. Netflix customers were outraged. They took to Facebook, Twitter, and message boards, sharing their anger and dissatisfaction. Not long after the announcement was made, Netflix CEO Reed Hastings made a surprising move: instead of forging ahead with his unpopular decision, Hastings posted a short blog post on the Netflix website, stating the following: "It is clear that for many of our members two websites would make things more difficult, so we are going to keep Netflix as one place to go for streaming and DVDs. This means no change: one website, one account, one password . . . in other words, no Qwikster. While the July price change was necessary, we are now done with price changes."[2]

Hastings could have hidden himself away, buried his head in the sand, and refused to change the policy. After all, businesses becoming arrogant about their products is nothing new. All too often, businesses will take a bad idea and run with it—only to have to come back later and pick up the pieces. But Hastings decided to cut his losses rather than draw them out. He admitted that the idea was a bad one and moved forward. In short, Hastings chose to listen and to be honest. Not only was his decision refreshing, but it proved to be the best plan for his business

FIGURE 1.1   Qwikster didn't live long thanks to Netflix's listening.

in the long run: after losing 800,000 after announcing Qwikster, Netflix gained a net 610,000 customers in the fourth quarter of 2011 (see Figure 1.1).[3] The lesson is simple: when you don't listen to your customers, you seriously risk losing them.

LISTENING BUILDS RELATIONSHIPS

I went on enough first dates in my twenties to learn about how listening can make or break relationships. A first date is very similar to a first business interaction with a prospect, potential partner, or colleague: both parties size each other up, trying to quickly determine if there's chemistry. The better you listen in that first interaction (and in every subsequent interaction, for that matter), the better you can understand the other party, get to know his or her wants and needs, find common ground, and create chemistry.

When people feel listened to—in dating, in business, and in life—they open up to you, which in turn helps a real relationship form.

LISTENING TO PROSPECTS VERSUS CUSTOMERS VERSUS COLLEAGUES

Listening to prospects enables you to understand what problems and pain points they have so that you can solve them with your product or service. Moreover, it helps you build an initial relationship—we all know that people do business with people they know, like, and trust, and listening is essential in building up likeability and trust. Listening to customers helps you continue that relationship, but it also helps you understand how you can deliver more to them and what changes you may need to make to your products and services. Listening to colleagues and employees allows you to build the culture of your organization, make it better, understand what holes need to be filled, and help everyone on the team feel important.

BUILD-A-BEAR LISTENS TO EVERYONE—EVEN KIDS

Maxine Clark, founder and CEO of Build-A-Bear Workshop, is an avid listener. Clark firmly believes in the business value of listening to her customers because, at the end of the day, their opinions are what drive sales. Since the early days of Build-A-Bear, Clark has had an advisory board made up entirely of kids. The members of the Cub Advisory Board, as it's called, are always willing to offer up their opinions about Build-A-Bear products. Clark uses the input of her child board members and customers in general to find out where to open new stores, which products to create next, and which products to discontinue. Because she is such an avid listener, Clark has developed a keen attention to detail. For example, Build-A-Bear's teddy bear sneakers are equipped with tread bottoms for traction, and the miniature teddy bear binoculars are actually functional. Those might seem like minor details and extra expenses to us adults, but to a child, they make all the difference in the world.

Clark listens to her employees as well. She encourages her associates to try new and creative things all the time, because there's no telling whose big idea is going to pay off. When Build-A-Bear gets ready to launch a new product, Clark contacts the stores with the highest new-product-launch sales rates and asks for input and advice to relay to the rest of the team. Clark's commitment to listening is evident in her business results. Over 60 percent of Build-A-Bear customers are repeat customers who plan their visits in advance, and the 400 Build-A-Bear locations worldwide brought in over $394 million in 2011. That's quite a price tag to put on listening.

Big brands like Build-A-Bear aren't the only companies that believe in listening. Vincent Cannariato is the CEO of Vincent Limousine, a national yet boutiquelike, very-high-end ground transportation service. Vinnie told me of listening, "I listen to the input of our clients, because they know better than me. A good manager doesn't know the answers; a good manager asks the right questions to the right people. No one can know everything. I don't expect all my managers to know everything, but I do expect them to ask the right questions to the right people, and then sit back and listen. That's where the answers lie."

THE ART OF LISTENING

Is listening in business an art, a science, or both? Richard Levychin is the managing partner of KBL, a New York City accounting firm that has worked with Fortune 500 companies, nonprofits, and small businesses. Richard leads KBL's pitches and, through the years, has developed a practice he calls "the art of listening": "'Listening to someone' requires that you 'hear' what they say to you and be able to repeat it back to them if not exactly, then in a format that provides a clear understanding of what they said."

"Listening to someone" goes much deeper than that. It involves using all your senses when engaging with others. It includes the ability to read and interpret body language accurately—taking people in and feeling them internally. It requires being extremely present to people as individuals and to the environment that they have created around themselves, which includes their own culture and makeup and the culture and makeup of their business. Finally, it requires taking the information amassed from these processes, internalizing all the information, and assessing and interpreting it in a way that causes you to be able to truly read people so that you can create the relationship that you desire with them.

Richard further breaks down the art of listening into four components: research, feeling, intimacy, and mirroring.

Research means getting as much background information as possible on the person and company you'll be meeting with. This might not sound like it's related to listening, but the truth is, the more prepared you are for an interaction, the more you can practice focused listening when the interaction occurs. As you perform your research, identify potential intimacy areas, which may not play a huge role in the company's success or failure but which are central to the company's culture or personally important to the individual you're meeting with—issues such as diversity, a paperless office environment, flexible schedules for working parents, or a favorite charity the company supports.

Feeling means listening to how you feel when the person is speaking. Are you excited by the person's presentation? Suspicious of what she or he is saying to you? Uncomfortable for reasons you cannot quite put into words? Listen with your gut, keep asking questions, and keep experiencing what the person has to say.

Closely aligned with feeling, creating and maintaining intimacy is very important to the listening process. Look for common areas that you can speak about intimately and in detail—ideally, areas that are related to the business. You don't need a lot of areas, just a couple. Consider giving up intimate knowledge about yourself briefly; then sit back and continue listening as your conversation partner opens up in response. The intimate feelings that you create have to be authentic, not canned.

Finally, the act of mirroring involves showing the other party that you are truly listening, reflecting back what you're hearing not only with words but with tone and body language. Nonverbal cues may account for as much as 90 percent of any communication, and so the value of mirroring cannot be overstated.

When I asked Richard for business examples of the art of listening in action, he said, "Pretty much every client we've won is a result of this process. I attribute the huge success of our firm to the art of listening."

LISTEN LIKE CHILDREN
WATCH TELEVISION

Dr. Gerald D. Bell, founder and CEO of Bell Leadership Institute and a professor at the University of North Carolina's Kenan-Flagler Business School, has over 40 years of experience working with top business leaders. He has seen firsthand the impact great listening skills have. Said Bell, "When you listen to people, they feel valued, respected, happy, and productive. They feel more motivated, inspired, and eager to solve problems and produce good results." He also notes the effects of poor listening skills. "When we don't listen to people, they feel hurt, rejected, demeaned, disrespected, and de-motivated."[4] Simply put, listening skills can make or break any interaction in business (or relationships).

After conducting years of research on the most effective and least effective traits of leaders, Bell advises leaders to "listen like children watch TV." Children sit up straight, slightly leaning into the TV. Their eyes are glued to the screen. Bell calls it the Achiever Listening position, and he recommends it as a first step in improving your listening skills.[5] When my daughter is watching the Disney Channel, I could be jumping up and down right in front of her and she wouldn't notice. Can you listen as intently as my daughter watches *The Wizards of Waverly Place*?

LISTENING AT SCALE
THROUGH SOCIAL MEDIA

Larger companies have always struggled with how to listen at scale. After all, in the past you could really listen to only one person at a time. Perhaps if you organized a focus group, you could listen to dozens of people in one day. But with the arrival of social media, for the first time, organizations can listen to hundreds, thousands, or millions of people at once.

Your prospects and customers are on Twitter, Facebook, LinkedIn, and other social networks right now. It's your job to find them, listen to them, and then engage. If you don't believe me, take a few minutes now, go to Twitter.com, and enter into the search bar the name of your company, product, or category. If you work for a large company, enter the name of your company and the words "I wish." If yours is a small company, enter the name of a product or what you do. For instance, if you're a dentist, enter the words "dentist" and "looking for." You'll find lots of people talking right now about you, your competitors, your products, and your services. Now, depending on your resources, you can join the conversation and keep listening and engaging with dozens, hundreds, or thousands of people each day.

IBM is an American multinational computer, technology, and IT consulting firm—the world's fourth-largest technology company and the second-most-valuable global brand. In an interview with eMarketer.com, Ed Linde II, who works on the IBM website team, described the formal steps that a company as huge as IBM has taken to listen to customers and prospects on the social web. Said Linde:

> We also have a program called Listening for Leads, where we have people called "seekers" who on a voluntary basis go to particular social media sites where they listen to conversations and determine whether there's a potential sales opportunity. . . . Seekers listen to and look at conversations. For example, if someone says, "I'm looking to replace my old server" or "Does anyone have any recommendations on what kind of storage device will work in this type of situation?" or "I'm about to issue an RFP; does anyone have a sample RFP I could work from?" Those are all pretty good clues that someone's about to buy something or start the buying process. We try to identify those leads, get them to a lead development rep who is a telephone sales rep who has been trained to have a conversation with the lead to qualify and validate the opportunity. They'll qualify and validate it and then pass it to the appropriate sales resource to follow up . . . I would say Listening for Leads has been our best initiative so far. We have uncovered millions of dollars' worth of sales leads

through our intelligent listening program and we've closed a lot of business and we expect to do more. That's going to be a big growth area.[6]

According to Linde, IBM has uncovered "millions of dollars' worth of sales leads" through its social listening program. It's not just listening for customers talking about IBM; it's listening for people using key phrases and words that identify them as great potential customers.

While you may not have the resources to do this level of listening, surely you can dedicate some resources to getting your share of the pie. Remember, it's not just leads you're listening for. It's potential problems or challenges with your products or services; it's customer sentiment; it's customer questions; it's what people are saying about your competition. Depending on how big your company or brand is, there is a virtually limitless number of conversations and topics that you can tap into.

WHAT HAPPENS WHEN YOU DON'T LISTEN?

What happens if you don't listen carefully? Your competitors will, and they'll scoop up your customers and prospects, even if you have a better product or service. The market will change, and you won't be paying attention. Your staff and colleagues will feel unheard and start caring less, and your culture will suffer. No matter how amazing your product is or how great your ideas are, business is about people; and if you can't listen to people, nothing else will matter.

BLOCKBUSTER DIDN'T LISTEN

Dr. Natalie Petouhoff is a business strategist who has spent her career studying how businesses interact with their customers and employees. Petouhoff studied Blockbuster's plummet to bankruptcy to figure out the root of the problem. Her finding was simple: Blockbuster wasn't listening. "If we examine what was being said about Blockbuster in social media prior to bankruptcy, the negative conversation was around late fees," Petouhoff explained. "Clearly, there was something not working about the delivery of movies. Customers had to come in, rent the DVDs, and remember to return them on time. Or else the 'evil' late fees would consume their positivity around the brand."[7]

However, Blockbuster was either not listening to its customers, unwilling to shift its business model, or both. Petouhoff created a word cloud to illustrate the social media conversation concerning Blockbuster. The larger the word appears, the more often it popped up in conversation.

As Figure 1.2 clearly shows, negative sentiments about Blockbuster's late fees were driving the conversation. If Blockbuster representatives had been listening to the conversation on social media, they might have been able to spot critical

FIGURE 1.2 **Blockbuster wasn't listening, but its customers were definitely talking.**
Source: Natalie Petouhoff

issues before they exploded into huge problems. Instead, competitors such as Netflix and Redbox stepped in, and Blockbuster filed for bankruptcy on September 23, 2010. This business failure could have been avoided if Blockbuster had been willing to listen to its customers.

VERNE HARNISH, MICHAEL DELL, AND THE KPIS OF LISTENING

I had the honor of talking with Verne Harnish, the founder of the Young Entrepreneurs' Organization (now the Entrepreneurs' Organization), the author of *Mastering the Rockefeller Habits*, and one of the great business leaders of our time. Of the 11 principles of a likeable business, he believes listening is far and away the most important. Verne shared with me the legend of Michael Dell, founder and CEO of Dell and one of the best ever, if not the best, business listeners: "All those that have ever worked with Michael Dell, and have experienced him firsthand, have said he's one of the most intense listeners you'll ever meet. He just insists upon listening over talking. I worked with a Dell country manager from the Netherlands who had a meeting with Dell. He didn't say anything at all for 45 minutes. When he finally spoke, he asked one question that simply cut through the BS."

Verne went on to tell me he's seen a direct correlation between the experience level of listeners and their ability to listen. He's even used data to prove this. As leaders mature, two specific key performance indicators (KPIs) can be used in any important meeting with a customer, supplier, or internal team. First, measure the number of minutes you spend listening compared with talking. As you mature, you'll see a rise in the ratio of minutes listening to minutes talking. Second, measure the ratio of questions you ask versus answers you give. The more questions you ask, the better you're listening.

Finally, Verne left me with a lasting analogy: Every time a leader talks rather than listens to his or her team, he or she is creating monkeys, destined to carry out orders rather than create, innovate, and problem-solve on their own. The more you talk, the more monkeys you get on your back. The more you shut up, the fewer the monkeys.

LISTENING: SOCIAL TOOLS AND PRINCIPLES

As your organization better embraces the tidal wave of change that social media and the new web represent, social listening will be at the epicenter of your listening activity. First, a personal pet peeve: let's strike the word "monitoring" from the social listening space. Monitoring is what the CIA and FBI do. No one wants to be monitored, but everyone wants to be listened to.

So how do you go about listening as you build a more social business? There are two categories of social listening: internal and external. Internal social listening allows for semipublic conversation among employees through a social networking platform. Two such platforms I recommend are Jive Networks for large enterprises and Yammer for smaller organizations. Both allow employees to easily communicate and collaborate with one another while allowing leaders to listen in and build a better company by using what they learn. Before committing to paid tools such as Jive and Yammer, consider using free tools. Set up a closed, private Facebook group or LinkedIn group for your employees and customers. You'll be able to listen to the conversation and learn from it.

External social listening is an immensely growing field. SocialMediaAnalysis.com lists over 300 social listening companies. Four I recommend are Radian6, Sysomos, Lithium, and Crimson Hexagon. What these companies essentially do is compile and analyze the mounds of data from Facebook, Twitter, blogs, and other social networks using any keywords you want to track. In other words, they listen for people communicating in social media about you, your products and services, your competitors, and your industry. And for large companies, there truly are mounds of data. With over 350 million tweets per day, Twitter alone provides massive data. What you choose to do with the data is up to you—but surely you can use the information to build better products, find more customers, and improve your brand's reputation.

If you have a small business, you can do external social listening entirely on your own through Twitter searches, Google alerts, and other free products. The bottom line is, no matter the size of your organization, going social means listening at much greater scale than you've listened in the past.

ACTION ITEMS

1. Think about what words or expressions you should be listening for in your conversation with customers, prospects, and colleagues. Write down a list of 10 things worth listening for.
2. Write down three ways you can better listen in face-to-face conversations and three ways you can better listen using social media.
3. Research potential vendors and tools for listening at scale using social media.
4. Write down five potential pitfalls of not listening better than you do today in your business.
5. Practice active listening. Start by spending one meeting listening more than you talk; next spend a meeting talking 10 percent or less; then try to talk 10 percent or less for a full day. Take notes along the way, since you'll be talking less!
6. Practice the art of listening with a prospect or partner: research, feelings, intimacy, and mirroring.

SHUT UP AND LISTEN

We've all been listening our entire lives, to one extent or another. Now the challenge is to focus on more and better listening in a business setting. Listen to your prospects, customers, and colleagues and truly pay attention to them all. Demonstrate empathy in your listening, and you will build real relationships over time.

If Michael Dell can go 45 minutes in a small meeting without speaking, we can all talk less and listen more to the people around us in face-to-face meetings. If IBM can generate millions of dollars' worth of business from leads generated from social media listening, then we can all benefit from listening at scale.

Shut up and listen, with all your heart. Seriously.

CHAPTER 2

Storytelling

Tell, Don't Sell

> Storytelling is the most powerful way to put ideas into the world today.
>
> —Robert McAfee Brown

I was at Andrew's Diner in New York City one day in late 2005 with my then-recent fiancée, Carrie, when we began talking about our wedding. I wanted a large wedding—huge in fact, as I've always been a public guy and wanted to share my big day with as many people as possible. But New York weddings are really expensive. We both had had extensive experience working in marketing and promotions. And Carrie had a genius idea. So we decided to create a promotion around our wedding.

We're both big baseball fans, and so we called up the Brooklyn Cyclones, a minor league New York Mets affiliate team, and pitched them the idea of getting married at home plate following a game. We'd secure sponsors to cover the costs of the wedding, and each sponsor would take part in the promotion before and during the game. Sponsors, and the Cyclones, would likely benefit from lots of buzz and media around a wedding with 5,000 guests at a baseball game.

Steve Cohen, general manager of the Cyclones, thought we were crazy at first (and in hindsight, perhaps we were), but he loved the idea and gave us a shot. Then 1-800-Flowers.com loved it and gave us flowers for the event, then Smirnoff provided alcohol, then David's Bridal added bridesmaids gowns, and Entenmann's added desserts; and then a dozen other companies got involved. In July 2006, I married my wife at an amazing ballpark wedding in front of nearly 500 friends and family and over 5,000 strangers. We raised $100,000 from sponsors to cover the cost of the wedding and a $20,000 contribution to the MS Society. As it turns out, the event did generate a lot of buzz for our sponsors. The wedding was featured on CNBC, on the *CBS Early Show*, on *ABC World News Tonight*, as well as in the *New York Times*, and hundreds of other linear and new media outlets. We ended up with not only a dream wedding, but a dream promotion: all told, we calculated about $20 million worth of earned media for our sponsors.

A few weeks after the wedding, we began getting calls from our vendors, thanking us for the buzz and asking what we were going to do next. Since we couldn't get married again, we decided to start a company around the concept of word-of-mouth marketing: theKbuzz, now known as Likeable, was born.

WHY STORIES WORK

When you meet people for the first time, they're complete strangers, blank slates—there's no connection, no reason to care about them or find them interesting. But then you say, "So, tell me about yourself," and you learn about hometowns, careers, and hobbies, all the basics that can begin to create a picture of a multidimensional human being. And when you continue your conversation, the absolute gems surface: the heartbreaking tales, the fun anecdotes, the childhood stories, and you begin to feel like you really, truly know the person. He or she might not be your new best friend, but you've grown significantly emotionally invested.

When you hear the story of how a company was born, or about the impact an organization has had on a customer's life, or about the unique experience of a group's staff member or partner, the result is the same: you feel an emotional connection with that company. Take, for instance, the story of Ben & Jerry's founding: Ben Cohen and Jerry Greenfield grew up in the same town on Long Island (in New York) and struck up a friendship in gym class in junior high school. During high school, Ben drove an ice cream truck. After attending and leaving several colleges, he dropped out to teach pottery and make ice cream on a farm in the Adirondacks. Jerry left New York for Ohio to attend college at Oberlin, where he too had experience serving ice cream. The pair eventually reunited in Saratoga Springs, becoming roommates and potential business partners. In 1978, after taking a course on the art of ice cream making, the duo decided to open up their own business. They discovered that one of the only college towns without an ice cream shop was Burlington, Vermont. So with $8,000 in savings and a $4,000 loan, they leased an old gas station in Burlington, purchased supplies and equipment, and began crafting the now famous Ben & Jerry's unique ice cream flavors, all invented by Jerry himself, like Funky Monkey, Cherry Garcia, and Economic Crunch, which Ben & Jerry's served for free on Wall Street following the stock market crash of October 1987. That same year, the ice cream company hit sales of $32 million, less than 10 years after its humble start.

A huge part of persuasive communication, and communication in general, is storytelling. When you tell a story, it humanizes you and makes you three-dimensional. When you tell a great story, people connect with you emotionally and want to get to know you. You become likeable. The same principle applies to your business. When your brand tells its story, it becomes more relatable; and when consumers relate to your brand, you make sales.

Storytelling is a primal form of communication, connecting humans universally. Nothing connects us like stories—they engage us with an emotional appeal and shared meaning, leading the way to greater empathy and understanding. Narrative structure provides an ordering of the world and the people in it, shaping our identities and defining our values, letting us and others truly know who we are. When you tell a story, you create a gateway for understanding.

YOUR STORY MATTERS

Nine years ago, Angela Shaefers was diagnosed with stage four cancer. Faced with the implications of the diagnosis, she decided to write a memoir for her kids to remember her by. When she showed it to a friend, she was told her story was so amazingly moving that she should publish it as a book and share it with others. Angela was reluctant, doubtful anyone would care enough to read it. She ended up printing 500 copies, selling all of them through word of mouth. Soon after, she was asked to speak at various church groups and other organizations, and she suddenly realized how important her story really was. People would come up to her just to let her know how inspired they had been and how comforted they were, knowing they weren't alone.

A friend in radio then approached her, asking her to do her own show. Again, Angela was reluctant, wondering how she could possibly talk about her personal struggles all day. Then it hit her: if her story mattered, then everyone's story matters. So she sought out people who had inspiring stories without the outlet to share them, and then brought them onto her new radio show. One story particularly stands out for Angela: a double amputee shared his story of participating in the Ironman Triathlon. His journey resonated with the show's audience; many of us complain that our lives aren't what we want them to be, but he has to put his legs on every day to make his life happen. It was a story of perseverance, but also hope: he turned his struggles into something bigger than himself, helping to develop prosthetics for athletes.

The radio show created a platform for individuals who had overcome obstacles and found their purpose to inspire others. Now, Angela's business, Your Story Matters, strives to keep that same focus, spreading the word that "you matter," with the goal to change the world one story at a time.

Angela's storytelling serves as an example to brands for how they can connect with their communities. Storytelling has the power to form connections and cement relationships. The most powerful stories are the ones others can connect with, when the general population can say, "I understand that; I've been there. I can relate; I know how that feels." These stories come as a result of honesty and vulnerability. Everyone has a story; every business has something to share. Those that communicate effectively are the ones that are truly open about what their challenges are and what has made them who they are today.

On an individual level, being able to tell your story as a business leader allows you to understand who you are, what your strengths and weaknesses are, and where your character lies. Even if you don't share your personal story, just by writing it down, you open the door to seeing who you truly are. And often, when you take a closer look, you can discover the themes and lessons in your story that uncover your purpose.

Storytelling can be a powerful gateway to incredible opportunities. Angela herself was able to help others and do something she found she was passionate about. As she told me, "Life is totally different when you're living from a place of passion, purpose, and an understanding of who you are, where you've been, and where you're going."

At our first annual Likeable U conference last year, my friend Cary Chessick, then the CEO of Restaurant.com, had the pleasure of meeting Angela. So moved by her story and her business, Cary asked Angela to come speak to his team at Restaurant .com and help the staff understand that their story mattered. When she visited, Angela had people take an index card and write down one thing they had gone through and one way it had affected them, things like, "I went through a divorce and learned I was resilient." Angela then shuffled the cards and passed one out at random to each employee. The cards were anonymous, but just by knowing someone at the company had been challenged by something like a home foreclosure or mother with terminal cancer, the staff was instantly more connected. They came to realize they were more alike than different and were inspired by the fact that their colleagues had the strength to overcome such struggles and come to work each day.

Stories affect how we act and work with others. Angela believes that the corporate environment has especially missed the mark on connecting. And if we don't feel connected to those we work with, the people we spend most of our time with, then teamwork, productivity, and results are compromised.

Take the time to write your story, learn from it, and share with others. Storytelling is one of the most powerful tools to build and maintain any relationship.

DO YOUR CUSTOMERS KNOW THE STORY OF HOW YOU BEGAN?

Brian Scudamore was a 19-year-old college kid sitting in a McDonald's drive-through when he came up with the idea for what was then called the "Rubbish Boys," a customer-based junk removal service that traveled around Vancouver removing unwanted items from people's homes. In 1999, the company changed its name from the Rubbish Boys to 1-800-GOT-JUNK? Within five years, what started as a kid with a $700 investment in a pickup truck turned into a booming business with locations in most major metropolises across North America.

Brian uses storytelling as a tool to promote teamwork and grow his business, because, as he told me, "When people understand who you are and where you come from, they're more likely to rally around your cause." Every weekday morning at 10:55 a.m. sharp, Brian and the entire 1-800-GOT-JUNK? team get together for a seven-minute huddle, a practice they've kept since 2003. Employees share good news, stories, and ideas. Not only do the huddles provide a place where team members can get to know one another and connect, but they also offer insight into how Brian grows his business. Brian and the 1-800-GOT-JUNK? team have a "Painted Picture," a single sheet of paper, front and back, that outlines exactly what the company will look like in four years. The Painted Picture details everything from goals to strategies for 1-800-GOT-JUNK?'s continued success and tells the story of where the company is going. This story is told in present tense; rather than offering wishful thinking, Brian's goal-setting technique forces team members to envision the plan as if it has already been accomplished. Most important, this story of the company's future gives the team something to rally around and believe in. Stories help focus your vision, offer meaning to your company, and give employees something to believe in and inspire their work.

THE MEDIA LOVES A GOOD STORY TOO

Nothing brings companies to life likes stories. They give customers something to talk about. Alana Winter is the founder and CEO of Stiletto Spy School, an organization that turns ordinary women into secret agents and superheroines by teaching them skills such as tango dancing, bartending, stunt driving, and knife fighting. Participants who attend the programs across the United States have an insanely adventurous time while also learning interesting and often useful new skills. Becoming a superhero is an exciting prospect and a compelling reason to join, and that is evident in Stiletto Spy School's business results. Alana explained that the key to making sales is telling a story to her customers—a story akin to a James Bond movie, but applicable to consumers' everyday lives.

"When I was little, I looked up to these characters, but I didn't have the confidence or the skills to be like them," Alana explained. "I wanted to grow up and go to a school to learn, and when I couldn't find something like it, I built one." Alana's story about why she founded the spy school resonates with people because they can relate to it. More important, storytelling is the number one driver of earned media for Stiletto Spy School. "The press is all about stories," Alana said. "If you tell a story to the media, it resonates with them. They want to write about it and help spread it." Because Alana and her staff are so passionate about the business, and because her clients consistently have such a great experience, many people are telling the Stiletto Spy School story at any given time.

Stories stick. If I think back to last month, I can't tell you what I wore or about a meal I ate, but I can tell you a story I heard. Your customers won't remember your financial figures or fancy product features, but they will remember your brand's story and what it means to them.

Vinnie, my friend from Vincent Limousine, shared with me a story about the first time he drove a customer in one of his limos, back when he first started his company. The customer happened to be Phillip Knight, the chairman of Nike. Knight was living in Museum Tower, a condo that Vinnie was hoping would select his company to be the house service, and so Vinnie was particularly excited and eager to do a great job. Knight climbed into the limo, and Vinnie began to drive him out to Teterboro Airport in New Jersey. Halfway through the trip, Vinnie looked back and suddenly realized that Knight had fallen asleep. Vinnie panicked a little, worried about how he'd ever get the chairman of Nike to be his client if he was asleep. He wondered if he should try to wake him up but decided against it. When they arrived at the airport, Knight woke up and Vinnie decided to say something: "I'm glad you trusted me enough to be able to fall asleep. I hope that you enjoyed your service and that you'll call again when you need a ride." And indeed, Knight did, becoming a regular client of Vinnie's.

This is the sort of story that stays with customers and employees, demonstrating the quality and integrity of service far better than anything promotional ever could. Vinnie is now in the habit of telling stories, recognizing that stories cannot be challenged, because they are always an undeniable experience. The strength of his business comes from the ability to tell a great story that resonates.

At the end of the day, if you want to tell a great story, you have to identify with your product, organization, or brand. If you do, you won't be able to resist telling your story—and neither will your customers.

HOW TO TELL A GREAT STORY

Author John Green's novel *An Abundance of Katherines* features a former child prodigy's struggles with adulthood, genius, and "mattering" to the world. The main character, Colin, also happens to be a terrible storyteller. Finding the extraneous details more interesting than his audience does, he fails to form a concrete beginning, middle, and end, leaves out the entire point, and doesn't give others a reason to follow along or be invested in the tale. His storytelling coach, Lindsey, tells him, "I connect the dots and then that becomes a story. . . . You see the connections everywhere—so you're a natural born storyteller."[1] Ultimately, Colin is able to tell an amazing story featuring love, loss, and, arguably, a villain, but more importantly, he proves that anyone is capable of becoming a great storyteller. As Colin realizes, stories make us matter to each other. Connect the dots—the ones between what's relevant to consumers and what's relevant to you. Just as in life, you need to find the interesting, relevant details, have a clear point or message, and give people reasons to care, to buy what you're selling (figuratively, but also literally). A great story brings meaning to a conversation and gives people a reason to care. You need a point, you need poignancy, you need an emotional connection, and you need a *moment*—the gasp, the sigh, the "wow," the "aw," the "oh."

Here's another story for you:

Anthony Ackil and Jon Olinto have been best friends since the sixth grade, after discovering the Massachusetts kids both loved the Boston Celtics and hated the L.A. Lakers. They grew up eating delicious homemade food from the kitchen of Anthony's Uncle Faris, a wise man who would give the two boys advice like, "Take it easy," "Live life," and, most of all, "Be good." The two friends had a dream to one day open up a business and work for themselves. Fifteen years later, they finally took the leap and started a business called "b. good" around the simple idea of making fast food "real," the way they thought it should be made: by real people, not factories. There are now eight b. good restaurants in the greater Boston area serving hand-cut fries and burgers made from fresh, all-natural beef from local family farmers. But Anthony and Jon don't advertise using the buzz words "local" or "all natural." Instead, they create a connection between their food and their customers by showcasing where their ingredients come from. In their restaurants, customers waiting in line for some fries can actually see a picture of Frank, a third-generation farmer who grows the potatoes they're about to eat.

Anthony and Jon have let customers help create the brand by making them a part of the stories they tell. Just before the first b. good location opened in January 2004, they held a contest to name one of their burgers; the winner was to receive that burger free for life. Inspired by a Brady Bunch character, the burger was called the "Cousin Oliver," representing, as the winner explained, "the new thing in your life that you're not quite sure of at first but quickly learn to love." At b. good, you can also find framed pictures celebrating other champion customers, including the winner of the company's 7th Annual Garlicky-Greens Eating Championship, a 95-pound vegan math teacher named Spinach Pi who swallowed 2.25 pounds of garlicky greens in 5 minutes, a feat that, in Anthony and Jon's words, made her "the greatest sautéed spinach eater on Earth."

When the two best friends started b. good, they didn't have any money to spend on marketing, and so they told their stories in a nonpromotional way. This began with self-deprecating e-mail newsletters from the two 25-year-old guys making fun of each other. The only thing that's changed in the past few years is that they now have an audience of 25,000 people and high e-mail open rates. From the beginning, they've always been two guys who just wanted to tell their stories—including ones they never should have told, like getting arrested at a concert when they were younger. But by telling honest stories that their audience cares about, b. good has developed a loyal family of customers.

One of my favorite stories involves their 1979 Chevy El Camino and how it got its name. Growing up, Anthony and Jon desperately wanted an El Camino. After they finally started earning money from b. good, they bought one for $1,000. They then decided to have it tricked out by a local street artist with a custom paint job of flames, b. good logos, and Uncle Faris's likeness. After they created the "greatest company vehicle ever owned," they realized they needed a name for their stunning Spanish half car–half truck. So, naturally, they turned to their customers, this time awarding the winner the keys to the car for a weekend.

The car was named "El Tio Superfly Clown Destroyer," or "El Tio" for short (see Figure 2.1). According to the triumphant cus-

FIGURE 2.1   **b. good's legendary El Tio—El Tio has quite a story to tell.**
Source: Jon Olinto

tomer, Dan, who coined the winning name, each word has its own special meaning:

El Tio: the crazy uncle, like Faris, that we all have but few of us acknowledge, along with a shout-out to the El Camino's "authentic" Hispanic roots.
Superfly: harkening back to the 70s' roots, when pimping was cool and life was easy.
Clown: McDonald's, the company b. good is in the process of putting out of business.
Destroyer: what b. good is doing to both McDonald's and all the other unhealthy fast-food places out there. And it evokes a great piece of Americana: the 1970s' gas guzzlers that came out of Detroit, the El Camino being the "best" of the bunch, paving the way for foreign dominance in the U.S. automobile market.

During his weekend with El Tio, Dan said he cruised around town with his girlfriend and handed out b. good's "healthy fries to the poor unfortunate souls who've never experienced the pleasure." What nobody expected was that Dan would end up becoming a member of the b. good family and a significant investor in the company.

EVERYTHING CAN BE MADE INTO A STORY

Ocean Spray was founded in 1930 by three cranberry growers who wanted to sell juice and fruit products. Their first product was jellied cranberry sauce, followed shortly by cranberry juice cocktail. Ocean Spray is made up of over 600 growers across the United States and Canada, and each grower has a story. Ocean Spray tells the story of its farmers on its commercials and in small feature videos on its website. The videos offer a glimpse into the life of a cranberry or citrus farmer. Gary Garretson, for instance, is a fourth-generation cranberry grower who says that his favorite part of the job in this day and age is having the opportunity to interact with the natural environment in a more unique way than most people are able to. Thomas Gant and his two sons, Steve and Gary, operate Gant farms in Oregon. The family is also part of the Ocean Spray co-op, and though Thomas is over 80 years old, his two sons are still trying to keep up. "If we can do half of what he does when we're his age, we'll be doing well," Steve says.[2] Ocean Spray employees may not spend all their time rescuing puppies, and their CEO may not have climbed Mount Everest, but the company still has a great story. At the end of the day, there are people behind every brand, and those people create stories. These stories are what humanize the brand.

Find your company's stories, the tales that bring it to life. Start with your employees: How did they start at your company? What do they love most about working there? How have their lives been changed as a result of their employment? What are their favorite work experiences?

Each and every customer has a story to tell too. Look to your most passionate customers or the ones who have had a significant interaction with your company. After you've found them, give them the motivation, tools, and opportunity to share their stories. With just a little recognition or encouragement, you can prompt those customers to share their experiences and potentially spark a movement of storytelling around your brand.

TELLING STORIES AT SCALE
THROUGH ADVERTISING

It would be great if you could sit down over a cup of coffee with each and every current or potential customer and tell him or her your story—you gesture wildly, punctuating each point, as your listener leans in, captivated. But that's just not realistic. So you've got to tell your story in such a way that all your potential customers feel its impact while on the other side of their TV, computer, or iPad screens.

One of advertising's biggest nights is the Super Bowl, which, for many Americans, is more anticipated for its commercials than for the game itself. In 2010, the most talked-about commercial came from Google, a huge brand that doesn't generally advertise. The ad, a line from which is shown in Figure 2.2, sought to demonstrate how Google's search engine is an integral part of consumers' lives. But instead of explicitly explaining this with a complex storyline, interactions between actors, or a voiceover, Google told a simple story though just a series of search inquiries. The ad, "Parisian Love," is essentially a love story: a man studies abroad in Paris; he meets a girl; he takes her to coffee; he buys her chocolate; she calls him cute; they fall in love; he moves to Paris; they get married and have a baby. It is brilliantly simple, elegantly subtle, and emotionally captivating.

The ad demonstrates how to use the product without teaching how to use the product. It lets viewers know how the product plays a part in their lives without coming out and telling them how the product plays a part in their lives. It is relatable and poignant and creates an incredible connection with its audience. It doesn't say, "You can use Google to do everything from translating phrases to booking airline flights"; it shows you a story about it.

FIGURE 2.2 Google's ad tells a compelling story of two people falling in love in Paris.

In order to win over millions of consumers, you have to be able to engage them, catch their interest, grab them by their heartstrings—you have to be able to tell a great story.

STORYTELLING THROUGH TV COMMERCIALS, WITHOUT TV

We all know that television advertisements have in the past been the best way for larger organizations to tell great stories to larger volumes of people. But the Internet has significantly changed this formula. Today, social media and online video have rendered storytelling to the masses possible for companies without the budget to buy television commercials.

Recently a colleague tweeted at me to watch a video: "You'll cry for sure!" Indeed, I clicked on the link (http://bit.ly/ LikeableRice), viewed the video, and moments later had a stream of tears running down my face.

The video told the story of a Chinese family overcoming obstacles: an injury left the son unable to walk, and his father nursed him back to health through grit and determination. The only constant through it all was family dinners. The video was powerful, moving, and unforgettable. It was also a commercial for BERNAS, a rice company based in Malaysia, and it was a little over three minutes long (and worth three minutes of your life, by the way, so do check it out if you haven't seen it already). It's a story of tragedy, forgiveness, strength, family, and love, and it's deeply moving. What it is not is a cheesy jingle or spokesperson telling you to buy, buy, buy BERNAS rice. Jingles and spokespeople aren't as valuable as stories. Stories are our social currency. Realizing that, BERNAS decided not to make a commercial and told a story instead.

That story was way too long for a television commercial. But BERNAS didn't have to buy TV time to draw over 600,000 views online.

A great story can be told to many without TV.

NOBODY WANTS TO BE SOLD TO, BUT WE ALL LOVE A GOOD STORY

Businesses that are too focused on selling and not storytelling suffer because they don't endear themselves to their customers. Think about the salespeople who call you up just to sell something and don't try to relate to you or connect with you on a human level. Compare Google's "Parisian Love" with, say, a Bob's Furniture's ad: Two salespeople lie across mattresses and demonstrate lounging on sofas, repeating with an off-putting enthusiasm how much of a bargain the products are. Crowding the screen in huge block letters are the store's logo, phone number, prices, and product features like, "Raise your head and feet! Individual control and massage!" These nonnarrative ads, with flashing price points and shouting salespeople, offer no emotional appeal or meaning to consumers.

Messages focusing solely on selling are so much less connective and impactful. If you wouldn't shout at, berate, or repeat the same phrase to your customers over and over again in person, your ads shouldn't do so either. Don't be obvious; don't hit your customers over the head. Take them by the hand on a brief emotional journey.

STORYTELLING: SOCIAL TOOLS AND PRINCIPLES

Social media allows organizations of all sizes to tell their stories every day, without spending a lot of money on the traditional storytelling tools—television and radio. Facebook has increasingly suggested that brands use stories in their marketing, even launching a "Sponsored Stories" advertising unit that essentially takes your brand's status update and promotes it to your fans and their friends. Facebook's Timeline for brands, also new in 2012, rewards brands that tell stories through pictures and video.

Pictures *are* worth a thousand words, and the growing popularity of social networks such as Pinterest, Instagram, YouTube, and Tumblr support this. Your organization can tell its stories through a picture or a short, low-production-value video, and if the stories are compelling, word will spread. The beauty is, if a story isn't compelling, that's okay too! Since you haven't spent millions or even thousands of dollars on a TV or radio ad, you can just share a new story tomorrow and see if you do any better.

You can use your social channels to ask your customers for stories as well. Your customers will want to share their stories about you—the good, the bad, and the ugly—so why not encourage them to share the good? Make it easy and compelling for them to share stories, and they will. Consider hosting contests, for example. A little added value can go a long way on social networks.

ACTION ITEMS

1. Determine your brand's story or stories.
   Write down:
   - How did your company originate?
   - Why do you do the work you do?
   - What kinds of funny or interesting things have happened involving your customers over the years?
   - Among your employees, who have had their lives changed in some way by working at your company?

- What charitable organizations or causes does your company support?
2. How can you inspire and encourage your customers to tell their stories? Brainstorm three ways you could make it easier for them to share their stories about you.
3. How can you create new stories for your business? Write down three stories you'd like to be able to tell about your organization in three years.

SELL YOUR STORY

Storytelling is the most effective means of delivering a message. A likeable business knows how to tell a great story. As human beings, we have a need for stories. Stories help us make sense of the world and find meaning. Move your customers; make them understand who you are and why you are—why they should care. We're all full of stories. Discover yours and start sharing them.

CHAPTER 3

Authenticity

Just Be Yourself

I had no idea that being your authentic self could make me as rich as I've become. If I had, I'd have done it a lot earlier.

—Oprah Winfrey

What would you do if an employee stole $17,000 from you? When I spoke to BELFOR CEO Sheldon Yellen, he made it clear that his company's values are authentically his own and that he is "loyal to a fault," believing that we all have a little bit of good inside of us. He then told me a remarkable story about an employee who stole a swimming pool from the company. The employee had installed and invoiced the pool to try to avoid getting caught. When Sheldon found out, he immediately called the employee and told him to meet him at the airport the next day at 10 a.m. sharp. After Sheldon's plane landed, he handed the employee an envelope that said, "I'm sorry." Inside was a check for $25,000 and instructions to keep $17,000 for himself and give the rest to the government in taxes. The $17,000, Sheldon explained to his employee, was to go toward paying for the pool that he took from the company. "I'm sorry," Sheldon told him. "I must not have given you enough of a bonus last year if you had to steal from us. I take full responsibility." The employee was shocked that he wasn't being fired, and BELFOR higher-ups thought Sheldon was crazy. "That happened in 1995," Sheldon said. "That employee is still on payroll today. I believe he makes BELFOR better each day he stays with us."

Many people who hear this story share the view of the BELFOR higher-ups: that Sheldon was nuts to hand the employee a check. For Sheldon, it's just a part of who he is. "I am who I am. I am BELFOR and BELFOR is me," he explains. But Sheldon hasn't always had such a positive outlook on life. He grew up in an underprivileged family, and so it was hard for him to find the good in his bad situation. "I was blinded by my struggle," he says. "The more I succeeded financially, the more I was able to see. When I'm standing in a room with BELFOR people, I look at them and say, 'Don't give me so much credit for what you do. I get to stand on the shoulders of giants.'"

Sheldon joined BELFOR, a property restoration company now doing over $1 billion in annual sales, back when there were only 19 employees. "People were taken aback because I was the son-in-law to the owner," Sheldon said. "No one wanted to help me." In order to prove himself an asset to the company, Sheldon worked hard to gain credibility and learn the business. To this day, he believes that he should be the first one in the office and the last one out—and BELFOR employees work long hours—so he arrives at 6:00 a.m. and leaves at 7:30 or 8:00 p.m. each day. To ensure that his employees know how important they are to him, he writes personal birthday cards to each of his (now) 6,000+ employees.

In order to establish the right culture at BELFOR, Sheldon makes it a point to lead by example. "I've never asked any person I've worked with to do anything I haven't done myself," Sheldon says. "I've been on roofs, I've carried things they've carried on ladders, I've gone two days without sleep on a job site, I've slept and showered on the beach, and I've gone two days without food during a hurricane." Sheldon believes that BELFOR's greatest asset is its people, and he truly cares about them: "I feel pain when a guy's daughter gets sick; I make the hospital visit. I fly across the country to show up at funerals. I do it because I care.

That helps develop a culture of compassion and passion, and it brings loyalty to this organization."

Sheldon's unconventional management style has helped him gain more business than some of his headstrong competitors. BELFOR has made 82 acquisitions, often beating out competitors who offered more money. Sheldon says it's because his potential partners have the choice of more money or a sense of family, loyalty, compassion, and the drive to do the right thing, even when no one is watching. Most people choose the latter. "Our business is grown on Jersey handshakes," says Sheldon. (See Figure 3.1.)

BEING WHO YOU SAY YOU ARE

Being authentic means being exactly who you say you are. In business, authenticity means that processes are what you say they are and products and services do what you say they do. Your job titles, slogans, and advertisements are brand promises

FIGURE 3.1   **Sheldon Yellen is the same person whether he's in a meeting, on a roof, or with his children.**
Source: Alex Gort

that your business must deliver to your employees and customers. Just as no one wants to form a relationship with a person perceived as "fake," no one wants to do business with a company that seems inauthentic.

Authenticity is personal; it's unique. It can't be replicated or faked. It's you being genuine and sincere. Are you who your customers think you are? Do you believe in what your business stands for? Do your employees? Are your products actually environmentally friendly, or is that just what the label says?

An authentic business leader's actions reinforce his or her organization's values. If you say you put your customers first, then you better make sure you do just that. Amazon.com CEO Jeff Bezos has delivered on this promise. He has repeatedly sacrificed short-term profits by reducing prices and even discouraging customers from buying certain products. Similarly, Herb Kelleher, cofounder of Southwest Airlines, has lived up to his "employees first" policy by refusing to lay off his staff even when competitors were laying off tens of thousands of employees.

Fannie Mae's mission statement is, "Ensuring that working families have access to mortgage credit to buy homes they can afford over the long term, or that they can secure quality rental housing."[1] While Fannie Mae says it aims to help the struggling public, it had to be bailed out by the struggling public during CEO Franklin Raines's tenure. The company ostensibly works "to keep funds flowing to support affordable rental housing"; yet it couldn't handle the responsible flow of funds within the company itself. Riddled with accounting errors, overestimated earnings, and excessive bonuses, the bankrupt Fannie Mae forced a $200+ billion taxpayer bailout, failing to deliver on its promise to its customers.[2] How many other contradictory mission statements have you heard? How many people do you know who say one thing and do another? That is the definition of inauthenticity.

Businesses need to do what they believe in to gain the support of customers and employees with the same values and beliefs. If you start to waiver from your core values and identity, you will create cynicism or doubt in your trustworthiness—you will become inauthentic. Your employees should be authentic members of your team, believing in what your company stands for and championing your values.

Starbucks believes that the key to its mission of building a company with soul is the commitment to never stop pursuing the perfect cup of coffee. However, Starbucks' CEO Howard Schultz once compromised the Starbucks customer experience by putting relentless growth and expansion ahead of quality. In order to achieve record growth, the company made decisions that led to, in Schultz's opinion, the watering down of the Starbucks experience and commoditization of the brand. Schultz admitted and apologized for this mistake in a companywide memo: "I take full responsibility myself," he wrote, "but we desperately need to look into the mirror and realize it's time to get back to the core and make the changes necessary to evoke the heritage, the tradition, and the passion that we all have for the true Starbucks experience."[3] Starbucks brought back the aroma and comfort to its sterile stores and brought its focus back to the quality of the coffee. Now, the Starbucks customer experience has been restored, and the company is moving forward with a clear conscience. Starbucks learned the lesson of authenticity the hard way. The lesson here is clear: Stay true to yourself and you'll give your organization more opportunities in the long run. Stray from your true self, and you'll risk not only losing yourself, but losing your organization's strengths as well.

GROWING YOUR BRAND AUTHENTICALLY

Whole Foods' cofounder and CEO John Mackey may be described as "quirky" or a "free spirit," but he owns it, quite authentically. Mackey split his college years between Trinity University and the University of Texas, spending his young adulthood discovering himself, reading philosophy, and doing "what people were doing in the early seventies."[4] After moving into a vegetarian collective to pursue his interest in alternative lifestyles, he began to care about food, specifically natural and organic foods, and soon realized this was something he could make into a career. So in 1978, with $45,000 from friends and family, he started a store of his own, called "SaferWay" (yes, that's a play on "Safeway"). When much larger natural foods stores began sprouting up across the country, Mackey convinced Craig Weller and Mark Skiles of Clarksville Natural Grocery to merge with SaferWay; and in 1980, the first Whole Foods opened. They opened two more stores in Austin and then moved on to Houston and Dallas, followed by New Orleans and Palo Alto. The company rapidly expanded across the country and now has 304 locations and revenue of $9 billion per year.

Whole Foods is a mission-based business. The grocery chain has seven core values, outlined in its "Declaration of Interdependence," all commitments to the equitable treatment of customers, employees, investors, and suppliers, as well as to people's health, the food system, and the environment. Whole Foods' co-CEO Walter Robb describes the company's mission in its simplest terms: "One, to change the way the world eats, and two, to create a workplace based on love and respect." Whole Foods certainly delivers on the latter: the company frequently ranks high on lists of companies that are best to work for, and the health and retirement benefits are generous.

After a shareholder meeting in 2003 when animal rights activists staged a protest over a duck, the company reexamined its meat-buying process. According to the new Whole Foods Natural Meat Quality Standards, ducks raised for Whole Foods are prohibited from being mistreated. In January 2005, Whole Foods created the Animal Compassion Foundation to help producers evolve their practices to raise animals humanely. In May 1999, Whole Foods was one of the first U.S. companies to join the Marine Stewardship Council, a global organization promoting sustainable fisheries and responsible fishing practices. In 2006, Whole Foods became the only Fortune 500 company to offset 100 percent of its energy cost with wind power credits; and in 2007, the company was listed as the second-highest purchaser of green power nationwide.

CEO John Mackey is the champion of authenticity for Whole Foods, his personality one with the company's and the company an embodiment of Mackey. Opposed to executive overcompensation, Mackey pays himself just a dollar a year and refuses to allow any Whole Foods employee to have a salary of more than 19 times what the average team member makes. Given a choice between Whole Foods being very successful but people's health and diet being poor and Whole Foods going bankrupt and the world's health being vastly improved, Mackey has said he would choose the latter. Ultimately, Mackey is still just a guy working on finding himself. "People want me to suppress who I am," he once said. "I guess that's why so many politicians and CEOs get to be sort of boring, because they end up suppressing any individuality to conform to some phony, inauthentic way of being. I'd rather be myself."

BEING HUMAN

Authentic business leaders are viewed as simply human. They avoid corporate-speak and commit to being genuine. Warren Buffett is considered the most successful investor of the twentieth century. He's also uniquely humorous and completely authentic. A letter to his shareholders gives a glimpse into his personality and his approach to business. Buried deep within the letter are some great lessons for start-ups and established businesses alike. For instance, Buffet writes that leaders can't afford to dwell on mistakes and mishaps: admit that you were wrong and move on. Buffett's letter tells his shareholders all about a $44 million sinkhole that was the credit card product he urged GEICO to create. "GEICO's managers, it should be emphasized, were never enthusiastic about my idea," Buffett said. "They warned me that instead of getting the cream of GEICO's customers we would get the . . . well, let's call it the non-cream. I subtly indicated that I was older and wiser. I was just older."[5] Buffett could have passed the blame on to GEICO, but he took ownership of a problem that he created. Buffett soared through the shareholder letter and tossed in a few great one-liners, such as a suggestion that the cohabitation of teenagers would be a great solution to the housing market debacle as there would not likely be a shortage of volunteers. But the most remarkable aspect of the letter by far is how solidly and clearly Buffett's personality comes through. It's almost as if you're sitting with him in a meeting and he says, "Okay, let's get this boring stuff over with" before diving into the explanation of how money was spent. He doesn't adopt an overly formal persona. Instead, he writes in his own authentic voice.

Ultimately, being authentic requires acting like a legitimate human being. Customers want to feel like they're interacting with a person, not a machine or a cold, soulless company. In order to be warmly accepted by your customers, you must present yourself and your business as human, demonstrating a true personality. This extends to everything from your customer service to your client pitches. If your employees don't believe you're the "real deal," they won't respond positively, but instead with distrust and disengagement.

Politics is riddled with inauthenticity, much to the detriment of candidates. Republican presidential hopeful Mitt Romney has a well-documented history of being perceived as inauthentic and unable to connect with his fellow human beings. In fact, if you Google "inauthentic politician," Romney dominates the first three pages of results. If Romney loses the 2012 presidential election, his "plastic," inauthentic nature will be to blame.

A great benefit of being perceived as authentic and human is that you're accepted for who you are and given slack for your faults. People know that humans make mistakes, and so a human business leader or company is far more likely to be granted a pass.

HOW AUTHENTICITY BREEDS TRUST
(AND TRUST EARNS SALES)

If everything is out in the open, others won't feel like you're hiding something from them and will have no reason to fear being duped or misled. And when you and your business are personable, you're also relatable, enabling a connection to be formed between you, your employees, and your customers. When you are open and personable, you build credibility and establish a level of trust.

Rob Carpenter, CEO of Friendgift, a site that allows friends to buy products together, credits his company's success to his authenticity. On one occasion, Friendgift was competing for a multimillion-dollar partnership with MasterCard. Friendgift ultimately beat out the competition and won the deal because, as Rob explained to me, "They liked us better as people." Rob focuses his professional life on building relationships and relating to clients on a human level. Rather than coming into a client pitch with a PowerPoint presentation or business jargon, he sits down and has a conversation in order to determine if there's a good fit. "People can tell if you're genuine and sincere," he explains. "It's obvious when you have an agenda."

People do business with people they know, trust, and like. In order to gain clients and customers, you must be likeable as a person; and in order to be likeable as a person, you must be relatable and genuine. You must be authentic.

AUTHENTICITY AND VULNERABILITY

A major part of being authentic is allowing yourself to be vulnerable. No matter the person or situation, it is difficult to dislike someone willing to show vulnerability. Opening yourself up endears you to others. So it's important to take off your mask and show yourself as a human being. Human beings have faults and weaknesses. Human beings cry (albeit, some more than others). Now, I'm not recommending you start a habit of bawling during board meetings, but by showing emotion and exposing your faults and what makes you tick, you allow others to recognize you as not too different from them. Empathy is innate to human nature, and when people are able to understand you, they're able to trust, respect, like, and listen to you. In order to be likeable as a businessperson and to extend this likeability to your company, consider being as human as possible. You're instantly more likeable, relatable, and able to form a connection with your fellow human beings, your employees, and customers.

Jeff Pulver, founder of Vonage and the #140conference, recently gave a talk entitled "Being Vulnerable in the Era of the

Real-Time Web." During his talk, Jeff described vulnerability as finding a way to connect with somebody. "I believe that when we look to the evolution of the Social Web," he said, "we can never forget the fact that we are all people first. We have feelings. And yeah, your feelings matter."[6] Don't be afraid to expose your true feelings; they're possibly the most powerful tool you have for winning people over.

In an episode from the eighth season of the NBC show *The Office*, Nellie, the new boss at the Scranton paper company Dunder Mifflin, is constantly tardy, rude, and generally unlikeable. The staff decides to turn the party they're forced to throw for her into a miserable experience in an expression of their dislike. Yet when some of the staff discovers a fact about her past—that she went through a terrible breakup with a recent boyfriend—and hear her emotionally retell the story, with a few tears, they immediately become sympathetic, feel a connection, and regret their original cruel plan. The boss's ability to share her personal story and be vulnerable in front of her employees allowed her to be likeable, gain her employees' respect, and win the team over.

Being vulnerable doesn't mean being weak or wounded; it means being open and raw in your communication and self-expression. It means loosening your concerns about how others perceive you and revealing the things that make up your identity.

Reality television is considered by some to be just the opposite of reality: people as characters, acting fake and misrepresenting reality. Natural food chef, author, and founder of Skinnygirl Cocktails, Bethenny Frankel, is a reality television star who breaks the mold with her authenticity. On her Bravo show, *Bethenny Ever After*, Bethenny leaves few barriers between her personal life and the audience. She's extremely open about her vulnerabilities: the intensity of her career, her drive for perfection, her feelings of inadequacy, and the constant guilt she faces as she juggles being a businesswoman, mother, and wife. Bethenny allows arguments with her husband to be shown, is completely honest about mistakes from her past and her rough childhood, and is often heard voicing opinions such as the fact that she's "damaged" or that her relationship with her husband is not the perfect one everyone seems to think it is.

Some may say Bethenny's unique persona is a result of her being unprepared for sudden success and simply not knowing any better, but, in truth, her openness and vulnerability have played a significant role in the success of her business. She has built her brand on pure authenticity: natural ingredients, real women, and honest advice to empower her fellow females. Skinnygirl is the fastest-growing spirits brand in the United States. After being sold to Beam, Inc., in 2011 for $120 million, the brand has grown by 1,000 percent, and Beam has seen a 12 percent increase in sales.[7] Oh, and the premiere of *Bethenny Ever After* was the highest rated in Bravo history.

Bethenny has come to relate to and trust her viewers and customers as well, as she wrote in a blog post following the premiere of the latest season of her show: "Thank you all so much for watching *Bethenny Ever After* last night. It isn't easy sharing the intimate, personal details of your life with the world, but I've come to trust and love you as fans. You have inspired me, you have entrusted me with your thoughts and dreams, and you make being totally honest and upfront the only option."

For a true relationship with your customers, authenticity is the only option.

HOW TO BE YOUR AUTHENTIC SELF ONLINE

I recently spoke to a group of alumni from the Wharton Club of the University of Pennsylvania. The audience was mainly small-business owners and brand managers, all of whom were attending to learn more about using social media for business. At some point during my talk, someone asked about my thoughts on setting up separate Twitter and Facebook accounts for personal and business use. Many people struggle with this issue, but I'd argue that it's increasingly challenging *not* to mix personal with professional online.

Who you are online is who you are in life and vice versa. There is no need for separate profiles because "business you" and "personal you" are the same exact person. Or they can be. Otherwise, you're dealing with split personalities and double lives, which is tiring, unnecessary, and ineffective. Imagine logging in and out of different Facebook profiles all day, for instance, in order to keep up with personal friends and work friends. Too difficult, I say. It's much easier to be the authentic you all the time.

Some prefer to keep semiprivate online identities, carefully curating their digital selves and handpicking who sees what. But those aren't their actual identities; those are masks they wear.

Aliza Licht, senior vice president of global communications at Donna Karan New York, is exactly who she is online as she is in real life. With hundreds of thousands of Twitter followers, she still considers each member of her audience a friend, reading all tweets and responding to most, consistently in her own voice. She offers an honest glimpse into her life and career, sharing photos from shoots, personal anecdotes, and thoughtful advice straight from the source. She doesn't draw the line between her career and her personal life. This practice has allowed her to rise to the top of the PR industry and has gained DKNY a rise in connectedness to its customers and brand loyalty.

Social media provides a great opportunity to display authenticity as a business leader and gain credibility. In fact, in a recent survey, 82 percent of respondents reported they are more likely to trust a brand when the senior leadership and CEO are using social media. Today's connected consumers look to social media to determine who companies are (note: we deliberately said "*who* companies are," not "what"—in this case and others in the book, we are referring to companies' "personalities") and what they stand for. But just being on social media isn't enough; you must be using these channels correctly, and that starts with authenticity.

If two equally qualified job applicants were placed in front of me, one with a completely open Facebook profile with drunk photos displayed for the whole world to see and the other with a blocked account, I would choose the open one. Being authentic requires a willingness to share your true self with others.

Dennis Crowley, cofounder and CEO of the location-based social network foursquare, is a prime example of openness. An employee of mine once checked into her favorite trivia night bar on the Lower East Side in Manhattan and, in her tweet to @Dens, gave Crowley a shout-out for fixing the foursquare servers, which had been down earlier in the day. Not only did Crowley respond, but he mentioned that he lived in the area, recommended a few other bars for her trivia team to check out, and *gave his address* (around Eighth and Avenue B, in case you're curious). Most people, much less high-profile business leaders, are wary of sharing personal information about themselves online. While I'm certainly not recommending tweeting your social security number, Crowley's demonstration of trust and openness holds a valuable lesson: when you reveal personal information, you instantly become personable.

As you develop your online persona, be sure to convey your in-real-life self in your digital presence. Learn to embrace the lack of boundaries between personal and professional and online and offline.

AUTHENTICITY: SOCIAL TOOLS AND PRINCIPLES

When you build a social media presence for your business, don't let yourself get clunky or corporate. Remember that your social accounts are competing for attention not only with your business competitors but also with your followers' friends! The more human and authentic your language and tone across social channels, the better.

Avoid overly formal, lifeless responses to tweets and posts and remember to use human-speak—conversational, short, and sweet—the way friends talk. Put personal touches into your social media content, including humor and personal anecdotes.

Remember: your brand is more than just a logo. Consider taking a page from Comcast's book. For the Comcast Cares Twitter account, Comcast features the face of team member Bill Gerth as the profile picture, with a bio saying, "My name is Bill Gerth also known as @comcastbill. We are here to Make it Right for our customers." (See Figure 3.2.)

Let your fans and followers know that there are human beings on the other side of their computer screens. Consider

Bill Gerth ✓
@comcastcares
My name is Bill Gerth also known as @comcastbill. We are here to Make it Right for our customers.
William_Gerth@comcast.com
Philadelphia, PA · http://www.comcast.com

FIGURE 3.2 **Comcast adds the human element to its Twitter profiles.**

signing tweets, Facebook posts, and other social network posts with your first name or initials, which also is more authentic and helps your followers feel like they're really getting to know not just your organization, but *you*.

ACTION ITEMS

1. Evaluate your business practices and employee and personal behavior: is every aspect of your company "walking the walk" and demonstrating who you are as a brand?
2. Conduct an assessment of how much of your personality you display in the course of doing business. When was the last time you told a colleague or client a personal anecdote? When was the last time you were vulnerable in front of your company?
3. Unblock your social profiles. Review how open and expressive you are being. Is this the "real you"?
4. Focus on building personal relationships in your business life. In your next business meeting, forget the presentation and try to have a simple, honest conversation.

IT HAS TO BE YOU

Inauthenticity is cumbersome, ineffective, and, ultimately, a losing proposition. Because of the nature of the web and social media, along with the fact that everything is open and spreads, people need to know that the person they're speaking with is genuine and "for real." Being human and relatable is the best thing you can do to help yourself and your company build credibility. Being vulnerable may be challenging for business leaders, especially men, but your team and customers will surely respond to vulnerability positively.

Like your mom told you when you were making new friends in grade school: "Just be yourself."

CHAPTER 4

Transparency
The Truth Shall Set You Free

As a small businessperson, you have no greater leverage than the truth.

—John Greenleaf Whittier

Nothing in the world could have prepared me for what I suddenly faced as a cast member of a reality television show. The moment I got out of the limo and walked into the spectacular $30 million home in Acapulco Bay where *Paradise Hotel* was being filmed for Fox, cameras were following my every move. Two standing camera crews were following the other 10 cast members and me, and as I would later learn, no fewer than 1,200 stationary cameras were planted throughout the house. For three months in the summer of 2003, the toilet and shower were the only places where there were no cameras recording everything.

This took some getting used to. My first night there, despite the smart warnings of my good friends back home, I had way too much to drink. Surrounded by cameras and models, and producers eager to stir up drama, I drank 21 Captain and Diet Cokes. I ended up saying some stupid and embarrassing things I regretted and generally acted like a total idiot, with the world later watching on television (yes, your author did once say, on national television, "Show the new guy some ass").

I had always believed in honesty and transparency, but living in front of TV cameras for three months essentially forced me and the other cast members to embrace those traits. There truly was no place to hide. While it took some getting used to—of the 87 nights I spent there, my first wasn't the only one in which I said or did something foolish—I did get a lot better at living in front of cameras.

What I learned from *Paradise Hotel* was that honesty and transparency are a lot easier when cameras are following your every move. I couldn't say or do something and then deny it. I had to own up and be accountable for my words and actions. Just by being accountable, not only did I feel better, but people began to trust me more.

Years later, I still try to live each day—at work and at home—as if 1,200 cameras are watching. Of course, I still make lots of mistakes, but I do own up to them. I've found personal and professional transparency to be freeing and self-motivating, helping me ultimately to lead a better life. (See Figure 4.1.)

OPENING UP YOUR COMPANY

Transparency among employees is equally as freeing and motivating. When coworkers let their guard down, open up, and share themselves with one another, they're able to become more bonded and, from there, are able to establish a sense of trust among each other. A trusting environment breeds collaboration and investment, invigorates productivity, and establishes loyalty, ultimately leading to higher retention rates of staff.

No amount of money or perks will fully motivate your employees or win their loyalty. What *does* make them go above and beyond for you is building a strong, trusting relationship, and that requires eliminating the walls between you and them. Let them know who you are and where you're coming from by sharing something about your background or vision. Unveil information about the company's performance or the rationale

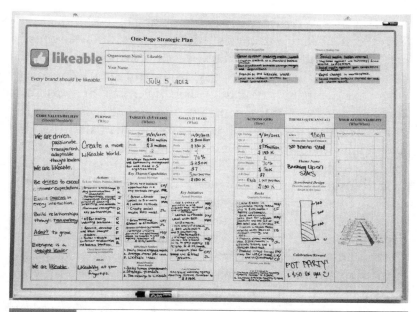

FIGURE 4.1 The Likeable business plan hangs on the office's wall for all to see.

Source: Theresa Braun

behind management decisions. Self-disclosure demonstrates to your staff that they've earned your respect and that you are invested in your relationship with them, which then allows them to reciprocate.

Take for instance, Sarah Endline, the CEO of Sweetriot, a socially responsible chocolate company founded in 2006. Since the company's inception, business has boomed to over $2 million in revenue. It's easy to tell that the company has a great product: the candies are wrapped in artistic packages. As Sarah described to me, "Every time you pick up a Sweetriot product, you see a piece of art." But the real key to the company's success is its transparency. From the beginning, Sarah knew she wanted to empower her employees and ensure that their roles were clearly defined, that they handle their specific tasks from beginning to end, and that they're never micromanaged. However, Sarah needed a way to keep up with her employees and make sure that they were aware of what was going on within the company. So she decided to make team meetings, or "sweetings," a part of Sweetriot's culture. Each sweeting features a look into the company's numbers. A company dashboard shows employees where the company will add revenue, inventory, and cash balance. Every aspect of the company and its finances are on the dashboard for Sweetriot's employees to see, and Sarah wouldn't have it any other way. Sarah extends her transparent outlook to manufacturers, trying to give them as much information as possible to ensure that the shipments go out as planned and that the product continues to be successful. Sweetriot's transparent policies ensure that the team maintains its democratic culture and that no one is surprised at the end of the quarter.

Especially at a large company, transparency can be challenging to incorporate into your communication practices. However, to make sure that everyone is on the same page and that information isn't withheld, you can figure out a way to openly communicate within your company and connect employees. Of course, face-to-face communication, like in regular team meetings, is the ultimate transparent method of communication, but transparency can also be achieved by starting an online community where your staff is encouraged to frequently post and share updates.

Yammer provides businesses with a very valuable tool: a private social platform on which employees can communicate. The platform acts as an equalizer, particularly in larger firms, giving entry-level employees an opportunity to talk to C-level management and have their voices heard. The culture at Yammer is a reflection of the product itself. The team members have what they call a "culture of dissent"; if you have an opinion about something that's happening, you're empowered to voice that opinion. Smaller teams at Yammer make decisions collaboratively and include participants from outside teams to ensure that they aren't working in an echo chamber. Most important, the team doesn't conduct itself behind closed doors or with extra privacy. Yammer's transparency comes from the team's acceptance that everyone in an organization, from the bottom up, should be held accountable for his or her actions. Ultimately, trust and respect come from the ability to explain why you made a certain decision and from the belief that you should be willing to be transparent about your actions, weaknesses, and challenges. Yammer must have been doing something right, as in June of 2012, Microsoft set its sights on acquiring the company for over $1 billion.[1]

Transparency isn't just about implementing a system for communication; it's a philosophy, an entire policy that should extend to every area of your business. Being transparent guarantees a level of accountability in which each member of the company openly takes responsibility for his or her work and actions. The opposite is just as real: a lack of integrity and trust in your company is like a virus, spreading cynicism and a decrease in faith, motivation, and productivity.

HONESTY AS A PERSONAL POLICY

"Impeccable timing," I thought as I read the e-mail from my dad's caseworker, Lauren. I was in South Beach, Miami, with my entire Likeable team for a retreat, while my dad, according to the e-mail I had just read, was heading into inpatient rehab for substance abuse.

I was crushed. My dad had a long history of mental illness and substance issues, and I had always been transparent with my staff about it; but the timing of this latest incident really sucked, and I just didn't want to be a downer while everyone was having a great time in Miami. I talked briefly to my wife and business partner Carrie about it, as well as our management team and Theresa. I hoped not to think about it after that and to party with the rest of the team.

Party I did, and a bit too much. I ordered Likeable orange shots for 30 people, and when most didn't want them, I helped finish—all of them. Three hours later, I had a night reminiscent of my first night at the Paradise Hotel, only now I was a CEO in front of a team who looked to me to set an example. I was embarrassed and disappointed in myself.

The next morning, I addressed our team. I explained about my dad, not as an excuse for my behavior, but as a way to bring a bit of context to the situation. I said I was sorry for behavior unbecoming of a leader and used my mistake as an opportunity to highlight our company's core value of transparency. And then we moved on.

A few hours later, one of my newer staff members, whom I didn't know very well, came up to me and said, "You know, Dave, we all screw up; that's not a big deal. The big deal is when you're not willing to talk about the screw-ups. My last boss never would have talked about his personal life or a mistake like that. It's really refreshing to be working here."

I was still sad about my dad, and about getting drunk in front of the company, but I was proud to have established a culture where transparency is appreciated and expected.

If I hadn't said anything, people would have just talked. By speaking up and being open about what had happened, I was able to reassure the company and even feel better myself. When you're dishonest and closed off, you're weighed down by what you're hiding, but honesty and transparency can lift those weights and be incredibly freeing.

TRANSPARENCY IS NO LONGER A CHOICE

Some children develop a habit of lying. "Did you brush your teeth?" "Yes." "Did you take that cookie?" "No." Parents eventually pull the truth out of their children and try to encourage honesty, saying, "I'm going to find out eventually, so you might as well own up to it now." Even as adults, we think we're so good at hiding our secrets. But whether it's a mistake you've made with your company or a personal dilemma, the truth has a way of sneaking out. Maybe it's a look on your face or an admission from someone else. One way or another, people are going to find you out. And they're going to be more than a little displeased at being duped. Just as when an indiscretion can ruin a personal relationship forever, when it comes to the relationship you create between you and your customers and employees, any deviation from the truth can irrevocably erode valuable trust.

With modern media, information spreads more quickly than ever before, and scandalous news about a business travels at light speed. Companies that aren't transparent will be found out; there's no question about that. It's impossible to hide the truth, and so don't bother trying. If you're doing something you don't want people to know about, just stop doing it—covering up is not a fix. When you embrace transparency instead of trying to hide away the truth, you'll create an open, positive environment in which your company can prosper.

TAKING DOWN THE CURTAIN BETWEEN YOU AND YOUR CUSTOMERS

Laura Baum is the CEO of an online organization called OurJewishCommunity.org, founded in 2008. As the name suggests, OurJewishCommunity.org is a place for Jews to come together globally and form a community based on their faith. When Laura realized that many American Jews were not having their needs met by other organizations, she created OurJewishCommunity.org to bring Judaism to people where they are—online. The online community allows people to participate in various ways, including podcasts, interactive services, online seders, blogs, educational materials, and more. OurJewishCommunity.org has a $190,000 budget, half of which comes from in-kind donations, Laura divulged. For that reason, there is a great need for transparency throughout the organization. When OurJewishCommunity.org has fund-raisers, the money goes straight to OurJewishCommuity.org, and Laura and other leaders at the organization are happy to share their budget or financial information with investors and other interested parties. Donors are given the option of anonymity, but most people are happy to be associated with OurJewishCommunity .org. When the organization is offered donations or fund-raising from other organizations whose missions don't align with their own, Laura and her team at OurJewishCommunity.org have no qualms about turning the money down and telling their members about it. (See Figure 4.2.)

FIGURE 4.2 **OurJewishCommunity.org is transparent about its financial information.**
Source: Laura Baum

Laura shared with me her reasoning behind operating a transparent organization: "At the end of the day, hopefully you have nothing to hide," she said. "If there is integrity behind the work you're doing, then you have no reason not to share. You should be happy to share!" Ultimately, more people are going to be willing to donate money if they know exactly where it's going. It might be intimidating to give people access to that information, but it does help build relationships and gain support from your audience, ultimately working toward your business goals.

Being transparent doesn't have to mean being a completely open book (especially when the book is of the financial variety), but as a rule of thumb, the more you share, the more trust you'll gain.

Scott Jordan, cofounder and CEO of the clothing company SCOTTEVEST, describes himself as "transparent to a fault." To illustrate his point, Scott wrote a blog post about his experience on ABC's *Shark Tank*, a show that gives entrepreneurs the opportunity to pitch their ideas to big-name investors. After his appearance on the show, Scott received criticism for supposedly using the show as a PR mouthpiece rather than as an opportunity to grow his business. Viewers of the show also criticized Scott for being disrespectful and aggressive toward the investors.

Scott addressed both these claims in his blog post. He explained that first and foremost, the show was an opportunity for him to sell his product and grow his business. It was only after it became clear to Scott that none of the investors were interested in his product that he decided to use the show as a PR opportunity. Scott addressed his aggression on the show as well. He admitted that while some of the drama was due to TV tricks and editing, a lot of it had to do with him feeling attacked about a product he had spent 10 years of his life trying to develop. Scott entered the shark tank with what he thought was a great product and a reasonable business proposal. Unfortunately, he and the investors did not see eye to eye. Scott's explanation and account of the events turned what could have been a PR fiasco into a positive example of how Scott values transparency when it comes to his business.

Patagonia is just as open, unafraid to air its environmental "dirty" laundry. The company uses the "Footprint Chronicles" section of its website to allow consumers to see the environmental impact of its various products. As Patagonia's website says, "The goal is to use transparency about our supply chain to help us reduce our adverse social and environmental impacts—and on an industrial scale." Instead of bragging about how great and how ecofriendly the company is, Patagonia is openly showing what it is doing and expressing that it would like to be doing better.

Similarly, Domino's Pizza launched a campaign in which it took a bold position to address customer dissatisfaction with the quality of its product. In videos released by the company, Domino's president, Patrick Doyle, spoke candidly about consumers' lack of love for the company. The company documented customers' comments in online forums, blog posts, and tweets, such as "Mass produced, boring, bland pizza," and then aired actual footage from real focus groups in which customers said things like "Doesn't feel like there's much love in Domino's pizza" and "Domino's pizza crust, to me, is like cardboard." The videos also showed employee reactions, with their crushed expressions and comments like "It hurts" and "That hits you right in the heart." Most companies hide criticism. Domino's broadcasted it, took responsibility, and showed the extensive measures it was taking to get back on track and regain customers' respect (see Figure 4.3). With the next quarter's financial results, the company proved that its transparency, literally, paid off.

Follow Patagonia's and Domino's lead and take the same high road at your company: if you're doing something great, find a way to share it; if you're doing something you're not entirely happy with, admit it and be open about how you're working to change it. Don't ignore any elephants in the room; your customers can see them and will appreciate you acknowledging their existence.

FIGURE 4.3 **Domino's Pizza honestly revealed criticism and showed how it was making changes.**
Source: bit.ly/DominosPizzaTurnaround

NONPROFITS MUST
BE TRANSPARENT

Nonprofits are under more pressure to operate transparently than almost any other type of organization, and understandably so; people want to know where their donations are going. When individuals, families, or organizations donate money to nonprofit organizations, they have an expectation of where their money is going to end up, whether it's helping to build a new playground for underprivileged children or providing funds for cancer research. Chris Rovin, CEO at the WeSearch Foundation (we-search.org), makes it his team's responsibility to grant donors peace of mind. WeSearch is a service that pairs up each donor with a researcher so that the donor is always aware of what progress the researcher is making and where the money is going. "Patients always tell us that they'd like to be more involved with the research process," Chris told me. "They feel more empowered when they see their donations go where they're supposed to."

In these modern times, consumers are increasingly expecting open access to information. When they can Google just about anything they want to know about a person or organization, they don't react too kindly when details are purposefully withheld and barriers are placed between them and the information they feel they have the right to know.

TELLING IT LIKE IT IS

After Research In Motion (RIM) CEO Thorsten Heins took the reins of the company, he introduced himself via video with the same rhetoric that RIM had been repeating for ages about how everything was going to be fine. Wall Street reacted negatively, with stock prices falling 13 percent.[2] Investors were clearly displeased with the PR-canned messaging. Heins later clarified his message in an interview, admitting that there had indeed been a shift in the mobile market and that because RIM had not recognized it initially, the company had lost its competitive advantage. But, he said, there would be many changes coming, in both structure and products, to help counteract this shift. Stock prices reacted positively, climbing back up 3 percent. Investors just wanted an admission of the company's previous mistakes and a CEO who would "tell it like it is" before they could believe in true change for the company.

We don't have any patience for people in our lives who waffle or lie, and we expect the same level of transparency from businesses and business leaders. Consumers can forgive mistakes, but they're less lenient when a company won't willingly admit when it screws up, quickly apologize, and right its wrongs.

Paul Levy is the former CEO of Beth Israel Deaconess Hospital. In 2006, he started a blog called "Running a Hospital" in which he shared his stories and opinions, minus any PR spin. He posted personal anecdotes and private details about the hospital, including infection rates. In 2010, however, Levy came under fire for what he admitted were "lapses of judgment in a personal relationship" involving a female former hospital employee. He resigned six months later. Thanks to his openness on his blog, though, the scandal was minimized. His transparency may not have saved Levy from making a mistake and ruining his career, but it did earn him understanding from his community. Levy continues to blog and weigh in on healthcare matters, though the title of the blog has changed to "Not Running a Hospital."

Humans are hardwired to respond positively to displays of "humanness," and consumers are increasingly expecting humanlike traits from companies and business leaders. So to truly connect with and earn the trust and respect of consumers, you need to be honest and show that, deep down, you're only human too.

Authenticity will take you far; transparency will take you even farther. Being authentic requires you to be your true self; transparency helps to convey your authenticity. According to Maslow's hierarchy of needs, a person cannot become self-actualized until satisfying the more basic needs of food and shelter. Similarly, you cannot be a likeable business without first establishing a foundation of authenticity and transparency.

WHEN YOU LIE, YOU LOSE

When you get caught not being transparent, you lose customers, you lose sales, and, most important, you lose trust.

Remember the BP fiasco? On April 20, 2010, an explosion at the British Petroleum–owned and –operated Deepwater Horizon rig resulted in the largest marine oil spill in history. The spill caused extensive damage to the marine and wildlife habitat, the Gulf's economy, and BP's reputation. BP was accused of lying after an internal company document showed that its worst-case assessment of the size of the oil leak in the Gulf was 20 times larger than its public estimate. Internally, BP said the spill could reach 100,000 barrels per day, but when it handed the documents to Congress, the company claimed that the number was 5,000 barrels a day and that at the very worst it could reach 60,000.[3] Lying prevented proper action from being taken to clean up the spill since BP didn't want to admit how serious it was.

What's even worse, prior to the Gulf spill, BP covered up a similar blowout in the Caspian Sea. Had it not been covered up, BP would have been forced to inspect its equipment and might have discovered the faulty setup in the Gulf, possibly preventing the Gulf spill all together. As a result of the spill and the deceit that came along with it, BP lost over $25 billion in market value due to falling stock.

More than that, BP lost trust. The company's manipulation of the camera footage showing the spill, its slow handling of claims during the first few weeks, and CEO Tony Hayward's evasive communication and insensitive remarks (e.g., that the disaster wouldn't even dent the yearly dividend payout) further enraged the public. As a company that paid a big price for misleading the public, BP serves as the perfect reminder to always shed some light on your company's inner workings and never try to hoodwink the public.

We can accept honest mistakes, but we can't accept mistakes followed by cover-ups and lies. We're all human, and we recognize that quality in our leaders. When we hear "I messed up; I was stupid," we respond much better than when the message is a blatant lie like "That wasn't me; I didn't do that." Think about political scandals such as Anthony Weiner's mistakes in May 2011. Perhaps if he had confessed immediately, he wouldn't have needed to resign from Congress. When we hear about transgressions from leaders, the true disgust comes from the denial of the deed; a grudge lasts far longer when a lie is told in conjunction.

In the wake of Bill Clinton's 1997 scandal involving Monica Lewinsky, we have even been able to forgive our own president for lying under oath; presently, he is back in popularity among the American public. If we're able to move on from that, we can forgive just about anything—but leaders have to own up to their mistakes before their constituents and customers can get to that point.

Lying goes beyond obstructions of justice. Every time you fail to deliver on your promises to your customers, you've lied to them. Consider the customer who logs on to a company's website, orders a product, and then later finds out: "Just kidding! That thingamajig you wanted isn't actually in stock like we made it seem, but we already have your money, so oh well." The resulting confusion and anger that brews inside the customer is certainly understandable. It's not the mistakes consumers are baffled by; it's the unwillingness to be up front that leaves customers feeling hurt, lied to, and screwed over. Think about your friends, family members, and colleagues who have messed up—you still trust them; you forgave. We have the capacity to forgive and move on; we just need the transparency to get there.

TRANSPARENCY: SOCIAL TOOLS AND PRINCIPLES

In the age of social media, customers have higher standards for honesty and corporate transparency than ever before. They're tweeting about their political views and updating their relationship statuses; they expect companies to be just as open and real with their audiences. Make honesty and transparency an integral part of your social media policy. When you respond via social channels, ensure that you're being as transparent and honest as possible with your answers and explanations.

When you screw up and make mistakes, admit them openly and quickly using social media. By using social channels when talking about such matters instead of traditional public relations and media, you'll build a direct, closer relationship with your customers—even when you're telling them about how you screwed up! Try to use social tools to tear down the wall between you and your customers as much as possible.

You can use social media to maintain an internal culture of transparency as well. Post often on your company's internal social network or intranet. Use that same tool to set up "office hours" where you can answer employees' questions to the best of your ability, swiftly and publicly "within the company."

Social media has rendered the world in its most transparent state. Whether companies embrace that transparency or not is up to them.

ACTION ITEMS

1. Write down three things about your business or personal life that you haven't ever shared with your team. Share one of those things at an upcoming meeting.
2. Develop a system whereby you can open up the lines of communication within your company, especially between you and your employees.
3. Start a Facebook group, closed LinkedIn group, or Yammer network for your company or team, and set the bar for encouraging the practice of openly sharing information by being the first to share sensitive information in the group.
4. At a meeting, offsite event, or retreat, tell your employees one personal insight and encourage them to share the same.
5. Write down three things your company could be doing better and one way you can communicate this to your employees and customers. Share the information with employees, customers, and other stakeholders.

BE OPEN AND HONEST

When you lose trust, it's incredibly hard to earn it back. So just follow the practice of transparency from the start. There's no need to lie in the first place; consumers understand human mistakes—just be human with customers. We need trust to gain the confidence and safety net necessary to take risks, raise the bar, and push for success. Trying to hide yourself—your truths, your faults—is exhausting and does you no good. Trust me.

CHAPTER 5

Team Playing

There's No "I" in Team (or Culture)

Individuals play the game, but teams beat the odds.

—SEAL Team Saying

In 1999 DaVita, a dialysis provider, was called "Total Renal Care" and was on the brink of bankruptcy. There was no culture, no vision, no money, and no plan to turn the company around. The outlook for the company was bleak.

A new CEO, Kent Thiry (known throughout the company as KT), was hired to reorganize the company. KT did turn the company around, and surprisingly, he did so by turning around the culture first. He told those worried Total Renal Care employees in 1999 that from now on, they were "a community first, and a company second." He called them "teammates" and "citizens" rather than employees. And he called together 800 of them to vote on a new vision, mission, and values and to rename the company. "DaVita," which means "he or she who gives life" in Italian, won by a landslide vote. Today, DaVita is the second-largest dialysis provider in the United States. In fact, it's become a Fortune 500 company, and it's brought in nearly $7 billion in 2011 alone, according to Bill Myers, vice president of communications. Just as important, the DaVita Village, of which KT is the mayor, is thriving. At DaVita, "team" is one of the company's seven values, and employees take it very seriously. DaVita University, a continuing education program, offers a class called "DaVita Way of Team," a 3½-day program to open dialogue and explore how the team works together and to move toward creating new possibilities.

DaVita is also an extraordinarily democratic company. In fact, it has been recognized by WorldBlu for being one of the most democratic companies in the world. Getting input and buy-in from the whole team was a priority during the new beginning in 1999. From democratically selecting the mission, vision, and values to choosing the company name, teammates were heard and empowered. Today, teammates vote on everything from the company's environmental goals to office workstation setups. Just last year, KT created the DaVita Way of Giving, a charitable initiative that put $1 million in the hands of clinic staff across the country to give away to local charities by nominating them for grants. A total of 985 clinics nominated more than 600 charities, giving away $1.1 million. A series of check presentations and community service events followed.

Over and over again, DaVita's clinic teammates have reported that having the power to help in their local communities through the DaVita Way of Giving has been a highlight of their careers. KT has made the team believe that corporate social responsibility starts at home, by empowering and embracing teammates and by tapping into their wisdom. KT's vision also led to the launch of the DaVita Village Network—a program established to provide teammates (or their immediate dependents) with financial assistance for out-of-pocket expenses during times of crisis such as a natural disaster, life-threatening emergency, unexpected medical or funeral expenses, or financial hardships as a result of military deployment. Since its inception, the program has spent more than $2 million caring for nearly 300 teammates. The DaVita Team is a family—all 45,000 of them. They care for each other with intensity, learn from each other, and work hard to live the shared values for each other and their patients. (See Figure 5.1.)

FIGURE 5.1 **DaVita teammate Anurati Mathur brightens a playground as part of a DaVita Village Service Day.**
Source: Crystal Henning, Avery James Photography

TEAMWORK AND TEAM BUILDING

Vince Lombardi, legendary football coach, defined teamwork as "individual commitment to a group effort." It's that commitment to your company and its mission that determines your success. With a clearly defined goal, a team can achieve much more working together than individually. Think of champion sports teams: often the winners are not the teams with the best players, but the ones that work best together.

99designs is a graphic design company with offices in San Francisco and Melbourne, Australia, and a group of independent designers working all over the world. In total, the team comprises more than 50 staff members and a community of 159,600 freelance designers. But even though there are so many employees with such vast space between them, the team at 99designs has an incredibly strong community. The designers and staff members enjoy a sense of camaraderie because, despite the distance, they work as a team.

The teams at 99designs go above and beyond to maintain their strong bond. They have regular weekly meetings called "all-ins," where they touch base with one another to make sure they're on the same page. Every month, the teams converge at "all-in all-ins" to make sure that they are all aligned on the company's goals and mission. 99designs even features its own awards ceremony, where team members can nominate one another to be the "99er" (or employee) of the month. The winners go on to a monthly leaderboard, which culminates in the winner being sent to either Australia or the United States, depending on where the designer lives. The designers do charity and volunteer work together, host karaoke nights, and have a beer with one another on a regular basis (see Figure 5.2). The team environment at 99designs extends from the top down: CEO Patrick Llewellyn has hosted several barbecues for his team at his own home and makes it a point to meet with all his staff members one-on-one. And as Llewellyn says, everyone works on a level playing field. Everyone helps out, no matter

FIGURE 5.2 Although the 99designs team members are located all across the globe, a strong culture keeps them close.
Source: Lauren Gard

FIGURE 5.3 **Facebook's hackathons build not just great products but a great team culture.**
Source: Gwendolyn Belomy, The OutCast Agency

the prototypes were so compelling that he had to reconsider. As Facebookers often say, "Code wins arguments." Facebook rewards people who, despite being told no, still believe so strongly in their ideas, they push to prove the higher-ups wrong.

The company's culture aims to keep Facebook as nimble and fearless as a start-up and to fight against innovation-stifling bureaucracy as it continues to grow. "You've seen company after company that rose to greatness struggle with scale, struggle with culture," says engineering director Andrew Bosworth.[7] Though Facebook's IPO struggled in May 2012 and the company, as of August 2012, had lost half of its value, Zuck refuses to let Facebook have that same fate.

A CULTURE OF SUCCESS

Culture involves a balance of a company's attitudes, actions, and values combined to create either a positive environment motivating success or a negative environment destroying morale. Threadless founder and CEO Jake Nickell credits the company's what the task. In fact, it's not uncommon to see Llewellyn himself doing dishes for the team.

99designs has a work-hard, play-hard culture, and the strong sense of community has paid off; the company has an incredible retention rate and has lost almost no team members over the past four years. The clear vision by the leadership at 99designs has allowed for the culture to continue to grow as the company has grown in size.

Building a team of motivated, loyal members requires creating a workplace environment where employees feel appreciated, recognized, and valued for their contributions. But rewarding and invigorating employees doesn't require a large budget, and it certainly doesn't require an all-expense-paid trip. A system of low-cost rewards can go a long way, like noting periodic positive contributions with gift cards to local cafés or shops. But really, the type of recognition that sticks with people doesn't have anything to do with money. Your employees just want to receive recognition and to be thanked for their work. This could mean giving them an extra opportunity or responsibility that shows they're trusted and valued by the company. Maybe it's some sort of public display like appearing on a "wall of fame" or being named the "salesperson of the month." And often, something as simple as a personal thank you or a thank you note says all an employee needs to hear.

MAKING MISTAKES MEMORABLE

Some companies have found unique ways to build a solid team. At SIB Development and Consulting based in Charleston, South Carolina, Dan Schneider doesn't fire employees when they make a big mistake. He doesn't even yell at them. Instead, he has an ice-cream party. The company's first ice-cream party stemmed from an employee who failed to back up his hard drive and subsequently cost the company $1,500. Rather than blowing up at the employee, Schneider calmly approached him and told him to go buy ice cream and toppings so that the company could have an ice-cream party. "If I yell at everybody, they're just going to think I'm a jerk," Schneider explained. "But if we're sitting around eating ice cream, everyone knows why we're eating ice cream: because this guy screwed up."[1] Schneider's method is effective in that it's memorable; employees will reflect back and think, "We had ice cream last week. I better back up my hard drive." Schneider explained that since that incident, the company has hosted only three other ice-cream parties.

SIB Development and Consulting's unconventional culture doesn't end there. For instance, Schneider doesn't like to hear bad news after 3 p.m. His logic? In Schneider's industry, there isn't a whole lot that's time sensitive; and even if a problem is, the team probably won't be able to solve it until the next morning. The policy gives Schneider some peace of mind because from 3 p.m. on, he can go the rest of the day knowing that he isn't going to hear any bad news, and his positive attitude is contagious.

Perhaps the most unusual thing about Schneider is his solution to employee turnover. Schneider has a theory that all employees, no matter how happy they are in their current position, will always be searching for something higher up and better paid. That worried Schneider because employee turnover leads to expensive training sessions, and so he proposed a solution to his employees. Each employee, no matter what level, gets $50,000 for every five years he or she stays with the company. Schneider says that $10,000 a year for employee retention is a worthwhile cost, and the fact that it makes his employees happy is an added bonus.

These methods may be unorthodox, but having a supportive, driven staff is vital. Just as in a sports game, you're more likely to win when you have a solid team backing a sound strategy. Make sure you have a loyal and motivated team before you play ball.

PLAYING BY THE RULES

Running a business is not all fun and games, of course. Each company has a set of written and unwritten rules for employees to abide by. These rules reflect each company's values and priorities. Some companies, for example, place high importance on promptness; others excuse tardiness but care strongly about their dress code. At Likeable, I'm very open to meeting for 15 minutes with anyone at the company, but that doesn't mean anyone can just walk in my door anytime and expect a meeting. So there's a rule: request and schedule meeting times. No matter where you work, you need to make sure that you implement, enforce, and follow the right rules for your company.

At Amazon, CEO Jeff Bezos and his team put a strong emphasis on great customer service, but also on the value of the customer service team itself. In order to teach all the company's employees how integral the customer service team is to Amazon's overall success, each employee, including Bezos himself, spends two days every two years working at the customer service desk. This experience helps employees better understand the process and gain a greater appreciation for the team.

Just as necessary as determining what rules are important to your business is determining what rules are not. At every company Phil Libin starts, he eliminates one piece of unnecessary technology. At Evernote, he got rid of the phones. His thinking was that if you're at your desk, you should be working. And no one has missed the phones. The company pays for everyone's cell phones, and the conference rooms have their own lines, and so each desk is able to be free of phones and the distractions they bring.

Libin also decided to change the company's vacation policy, offering unlimited vacation time. Employees are free to take as much time as they want, as long as they get their work done. Libin explains that the company's yardstick for employee performance is the same, regardless: "Did you accomplish something great?" Other companies, including Netflix and IBM, have established similarly open or flexible time-off policies, gauging employee performance on the quality of work, not quantity of days worked. These companies have learned that the standard corporate method didn't make sense for their business and that, in fact, flexible work hours led to an increase in retention and productivity for the team.[2]

Evernote's company culture comes as a result of Libin routinely asking whether or not a particular policy exists because it's an expected default of "corporate stupidity" or because it actually helps the company accomplish something. Often, he realizes it's the former, and that's when Evernote just stops doing it. Great work can result from a willingness to set aside conventional, corporate thinking. Don't have rules just for the sake of having rules, and don't do things a certain way just because it's the way things have always been done.

NOT PLAYING BY ANOTHER TEAM'S RULES: A $500,000 MISTAKE

Just because your organization has written and unwritten rules for the way you do business doesn't mean your customers, partners, and vendors have similar rules. Learning to play not only by your rules but by *their* rules is essential in order to succeed— and potentially devastating when you don't. I certainly learned this the hard way.

In order to not embarrass them, I won't name the company or the individuals involved. I will say that for years our company has had a prosperous relationship with a particular Fortune 500 company, serving multiple business units within that company, netting over $400,000 in revenue in 2011 from it and—until the incident—expecting over $500,000 in 2012.

In September 2011, I decided I wanted to grow our overall relationship with the client and meet other executives who worked there. I asked our account team to reach out to the boss of one of our client contacts, a vice president named Bill, in order to schedule a 30-minute presentation on social media trends. I knew I could add a lot of value in those 30 minutes, and I was not planning on selling our services at all—just building credibility and growing our overall relationship. My team reached out to Bill's assistant to request a call.

Just a few hours later, I got an e-mail from Becky, the client contact. The e-mail read, "Call my cell phone right now."

I assumed there was a marketing crisis to deal with, as she normally didn't work with me directly, and so I cleared time and called Becky's cell. She was furious!

"How dare you go above my head to schedule time with Bill! You've been working with us for years. How could you not know how we do things here? He's three levels above your day-to-day contacts! What the hell were you thinking?"

I said I was sorry right away and explained that I truly meant no disrespect and just wanted to add value. I sent her flowers the next day with another apology. What I didn't say was that I couldn't understand why she was so upset—that I was only going to add value and make her look smart for working with us and that I'd gladly take a call with anyone who could do the same for me, without complaint or retribution.

The relationship with our client continued for four more months after that day. From reports I got from my team, everything was going great—we were doing good work with excellent results, and our various client contacts there were thrilled. But as the year wrapped up, it became clear that we were likely going to lose the company's business. In December, we were told that the company had consolidated social media agencies and wouldn't need our services anymore. I can never prove that we lost the business because of our reaching out to schedule that meeting with Bill, but nobody will ever be able to convince me otherwise, either. Who knows? We maintain an excellent relationship today with most of the folks we used to work with there, and the time may come when we again have the opportunity to do business with them. But in the meantime, it was a costly mistake that I made—and an important lesson: learn to play by their rules, even if you don't always agree with them.

LETTING OTHERS SHINE

Part of being a great leader is giving credit to your team and seeking none of your own. When praised, a great leader credits his or her success to the work of others and maybe a little luck.

Letting others shine is mutually beneficial: your humility is admired and makes you more likeable, and the person you praise gains motivation, appreciation, and a boost in confidence. There's absolutely no benefit to your company of you alone looking good or having a large ego.

In *Good to Great*, Jim Collins describes this type of leader as a "Level 5 leader," an individual who combines both humility and personal drive: "Level 5 leaders channel their ego needs away from themselves and into the larger goal of building a great company." That's not to say that great leaders can't have high self-esteem or ambition, but their ambition is primarily focused on the good of their company, not personal gain.

Collins uses Colman Mockler as an example of a Level 5 leader. From 1975 to 1991, Colman Mockler, the CEO of Gillette, faced threats to the company's success, including takeover bids from Revlon and a battle from investment group Coniston Partners to seize control of the board in hopes of selling off the company. If Mockler had chosen to give into Revlon, he would have pocketed millions from flipping his stock and cashing in. Instead, Mockler chose to fight for Gillette, acting in the company's best interest rather than his own. In fact, Mockler's decision benefited the company, its customers, and shareholders; had he given into the takeover battle, the projects Gillette was working on would have been eliminated, along with the future of some of its greatest products, and long-term shareholders would have ended up being three times worse off. Mockler's dedication to the company and moral compass ultimately saved Gillette and nurtured its potential to become great.

As the saying goes, "There's no 'I' in 'team.'"

THINKING OUTSIDE THE BOX

As important as it is to play by the rules, getting your team to think outside the box is essential. A study by Adobe called "State of Create" shows that 80 percent of people believe that creativity leads to economic growth, but that only 25 percent of people feel that they are living up to their full creative potential and that 75 percent of people feel that their employers put pressure on them to be productive rather than to be creative.[3] In order to succeed, a company must have creative thinking to fuel innovation. This won't happen when your employees aren't given the opportunity to be creative or if all your employees are trained to think exactly the same way. You need as many unique ideas as possible in order to find the true gems, and the best way to make people feel comfortable sharing their ideas is to create an environment that values differing opinions and encourages time spent on creative thinking.

"Don't do indoctrination, where you pummel each employee to think like the Borg," says Paul English, Kyak's cofounder and chief technology officer, referring to the *Star Trek* race who lose a sense of self.[4] Encourage your employees to think and act as individuals and be open to new things. English suggests that senior executives be measured on how much innovation their teams try each quarter. When it comes to creativity, we're inspired by our environments, the people and things we surround ourselves with. To encourage innovative ideas and creative solutions, build team environments that inspire members; creative people inspire other creative people, resulting in exponential innovation. Kyak has said that it hires entrepreneurial minds only. The company doesn't do design by committee or host big meetings, but it does reward risk taking and fast decision making, no matter the resulting failures.

The first step toward innovation is simply taking a first step. It's about starting something and taking initiative. Your company needs employees who will "poke the box," or take initiative to implement their crazy ideas. You need the ones who aren't afraid to speak up or do something new. If your company itself doesn't poke the box, you're at risk of continuously playing catch-up rather than setting standards. "The job isn't to catch up to the status quo," says *Poke the Box* author Seth Godin. "The job is to invent the status quo."[5]

Threadless has a "do-first" company work ethic. When Jake Nickell founded the company in 2000, he was a web designer with no clue of how to screen-print T-shirts, ship orders, or charge credit cards. But rather than being afraid to take a step in a risky direction, he and his team were confident in their ability to figure it out. "It's really easy to come up with a million reasons why you're not ready to get it done," says Jeffrey Kalmikoff, former chief creative officer at Threadless. "You just need to take that first step, because if you have that list of a million reasons

[why] it's not ready, by taking that first step, that list is going to turn into a million ways to make it better."[6]

You need a team of fearless employees. Hire the creative-thinking risk takers, the ones who will jump from an airplane but build a parachute on the way down.

In 2004, the creative thinker and risk taker Mark Zuckerberg started Facebook in his Harvard dorm room. Since then, Zuck has ruthlessly fought to preserve the "hacker way" and the intense, engineering-driven culture responsible for the company's incredible success. The hacker way is Zuck's approach to thinking and building that requires iteration, with no patience for the concept of "good enough." This philosophy helps to ensure that the company never becomes complacent or stagnant. The hacker way has defined the entire culture of Facebook. At Facebook, employees take to heart the messages with constant reminders to the team that "Done is better than perfect" and "Move fast, break things."

This culture extends to the programs and policies Facebook has put in place. On their first day, new engineering recruits start a six-week boot-camp program. It begins with a quick orientation, and then the engineers are sent six e-mails outlining a series of tasks to perform. This initiation ensures that employees learn to be empowered to confidently take initiative.

The foundation of the hacker-way culture is the hackathon, an all-nighter that occurs every few months at the company. There's only one rule at a hackathon: no one is allowed to work on anything he or she normally does—this gives the chance for Facebook engineers to try out their craziest, riskiest ideas. The hackathon has led to many of Facebook's most successful features, including, more recently, Timeline. It's a throwback to Zuck's Harvard days, a reminder of how Facebook began and how it will always remain (see Figure 5.3). In fact, Facebook's hackathons today extend beyond engineers, to sales, operations, and all employees throughout the now-public company.

At Facebook, there isn't *one* right answer; there's an infinite possibility of right answers. Everyone is welcome and encouraged to offer his or her own approach or idea at any time. In fact, dissent is actually encouraged at the company. Facebook Chat was initially repeatedly struck down by Zuck, but eventually

culture for its success. This culture is driven solely by the company's mission statement: "Inspire Awesomeness." Awesomeness is reflected in everything the company does, including monthly "awesome parties," DIY days where employees can work on anything they want, and a policy that allows anyone in the company to give any other employee a bonus. The policies have worked out well for the company, as Threadless has an incredible employee retention rate.[8]

A culture of success blooms when employees are passionately engaged in the business and driven by its mission, working with a sense of empowerment and inspiration rather than trudging through days of bureaucratic policies. Historically, companies with performance-oriented cultures with strong internal communication and an acceptance of new ideas and a healthy level of risk taking have enjoyed better financial growth. Today, it's not enough to just have a great product or service and robust financials; long-term business success depends on a healthy culture.

Greg Smith, an ex-Goldman Sachs employee, wrote a scathing *New York Times* piece about why he left after spending 12 years at the firm. According to Smith, the company's environment had grown to be "toxic and destructive." He credits culture for Goldman Sachs's success, a culture that had once revolved around teamwork and integrity, always putting the client first. "I knew it was time to leave when I realized I could no longer look students in the eye and tell them what a great place this was to work," he remembers.[9] Smith names the loss of culture and resulting decline in moral fiber as the firm's most serious threat to its long-term success, or even survival. Smith used to advise his trillion-dollar client base what was best for their money, even if it meant the firm lost out, but he's seen this practice fall out of favor over the past 10 years. He became dumbfounded by the lack of respect for clients at the firm: he attended meetings where not a single minute was devoted to discussing how to help clients and where managing directors referred to their clients as "muppets," displaying not one lick of integrity. To regain the company's integrity and success, the board of directors must make clients the focal point of the firm once more, weed out the toxic employees, and reinstate the mission-driven culture. When a company gains traction in an industry, it can get caught up in financial success and lose sight of its values and culture. As your company grows, be wary of forgetting who it is and what made it great in the first place.

Culture is where winning strategy is created. At 2012's SXSW Conference in Austin, Texas, business leaders discussed the connection between strategy and company culture. Howard Saatchi, cofounder of NationalField, spoke about how the company's culture of accountability made it possible to carry out the strategy to connect on-the-ground operatives during the 2008 Obama campaign.[10] Above strategy and above leadership, a company's culture is the true determiner of business success.

That's not to say that strategy and leadership aren't important, of course; but a team can succeed only if it's supported by a viable culture. Consider Zappos: the company's strategy is exceptional customer service. To achieve this, Zappos created a culture of happiness to ensure that happy employees led to happy customers. Research has even shown that companies with highly aligned strategies and cultures have a 30 percent higher growth rate than that of other companies. Ultimately, a toxic culture will cause your brand and strategy to perish, while a culture that nurtures your brand and strategy will allow your business to thrive.

XOOGLERS

Google has long been praised for its corporate culture. The company consistently ranks high on surveys of top ideal employers and was number one on *Fortune*'s list of best companies to work for in 2007, 2008, and 2012. At the Googleplex, Google's corporate headquarters in Mountain View, California, employees are given access to a recreational center with amenities including a gym, Ping-Pong table, bowling alley, and baby grand piano. Google says of itself, "We strive to maintain the open culture often associated with start-ups, in which everyone is a hands-on contributor and feels comfortable sharing ideas and opinions."[11] This includes weekly "TGIF" all-hands meetings and unique office spaces and cafés designed to "encourage interactions between Googlers within and across teams, and to spark conversation about work as well as play"—which explains office spaces that resemble a terrace in Manhattan and a pub in Dublin. In an effort to optimize creative thinking, Google instated a policy of Innovation Time Off, where employees are encouraged to spend 20 percent of their time on projects that interest them outside their core job descriptions.

Yet, in recent years, there has been a bit of an exodus from Google, and ex-employees (or "Xooglers") haven't shied away from sharing why: Google had lost its start-up-like, innovative culture, they said. After three years at the company, former Google engineer James Whittaker openly discussed why he felt compelled to leave in early 2012. According to Whittaker, with the start of cofounder Larry Page's reign as CEO in the spring of 2011, Google's once-great culture took a hit. He describes the company during the pre-Page era as "an innovation factory," with advertising revenue used to fund smart and out-of-the-box thinking. From this machine came such important products as Gmail and Chrome, "results of entrepreneurship at the lowest levels of the company."

The days of hiring smart people and empowering them to create great products were gone. App engine fees were raised, Google Labs was shut down, once-free APIs were given costs, and focus turned to the build of Google+ and Google's quest to dominate the social web. "Suddenly, 20 percent meant half-assed," Whittaker recounts. "The trappings of entrepreneurship were dismantled." Many of his fellow former Googlers share the same sentiment: the start-up spirit had been replaced by a culture focused on the bottom line. "The Google I was passionate about was a technology company that empowered its employees to innovate," Whittaker laments. "The Google I left was an advertising company with a single corporate-mandated focus."[12]

The story Whittaker and his fellow Xooglers tell is a cautionary tale about what happens when a company's culture becomes a casualty of bureaucracy: the loss of great talent, the loss of an innovative spark, and the loss of the company's essence. Part of Google's philosophy is "Great, creative things are more likely to happen with the right company culture." And when you lose that culture? Well, you'll have to settle for just "so-so, uninspired things," I suppose.

CULTURE AND TEAMWORK:
SOCIAL TOOLS AND PRINCIPLES

Internal social networks can be a great tool for team-building and connecting people at your organization who might not otherwise be connected. Creating a Facebook group, LinkedIn group, or Yammer network will unite your employees and build a close-knit, hypercommunicative company.

For example, at Likeable we've set up four internal closed Facebook groups: one for senior management, one for all employees among three U.S. offices, one for staff across the world of our global partners, and one for interns across multiple offices. Each group serves to help overcome geographical and other boundaries and gives people a chance to know one another on a much more personal level. People post birthday wishes, pictures, and funny anecdotes on the groups' pages, content that wouldn't be appropriate for "e-mail all" but in the social context is welcome and fun. And people can collaborate much more efficiently than before, getting their questions answered at times by people they've never met (and might never meet!) in other departments from across the world.

In terms of external social media, opening up access to your business's Twitter account to more people from your company will allow everyone to have a voice and interact with your community and customers. Why should folks on the marketing team be the only ones who interact with people online, when in real-life sales, folks in public relations and customer service have lots of opportunities to interact with prospects and customers? Make sure to also use social media to extend your culture and share your company with the world. Give your audience a behind-the-scenes look with photos or videos from your offices. Threadless, for example, tweets and shares Instagram photos of the view from inside its warehouse, photo shoots, and even employee pranks. And don't hesitate to recognize your employees and their stellar work. By extending your culture to your social media outlets, you'll allow the whole world to truly get to know—and love—your business.

ACTION ITEMS

1. Hold a team meeting and brainstorm activities your employees would enjoy as a team. Choose three favorites and write down a plan to make one of those activities part of your culture.
2. Write down the rules—official and unofficial—of your company. Are there any that don't contribute to your culture? If so, get rid of them!
3. Write down three inexpensive or free ways you can engender a better sense of team within your company or department.
4. Write down your eight key values for your company and its culture, and have your team do the same. Do they align? If not, hold a team meeting to establish a value system for your organization.

THERE'S NO "I" IN TEAM, BUT THERE'S AN "I" IN LEADERSHIP

In *Employees First, Customers Second: Turning Conventional Management Upside Down,* author Vineet Nayar argues that business leaders should put their employees ahead of customers, placing an emphasis on building a culture rather than first focusing on external sales and marketing. The truth is, especially for medium and large businesses, you can't really take care of your customers until you have taken care of your own team. By building a set of guidelines that allow for innovation, teamwork, and a strong culture, the staff you manage will *want* to take care of customers. If you can build an entrepreneurial mindset in your team, with the understanding that ideas and innovation can come from anywhere in the company, people will be intrinsically motivated to excel. No matter what the size of your organization, if you can build a likeable community, then that community will want to be likeable to the world beyond your company's walls.

CHAPTER 6

Responsiveness
Taking Listening One Step Further

Life is 10 percent what happens to you and 90 percent how you react to it.

—Charles R. Swindoll

On a particularly springlike Sunday afternoon in May 2011, the Emerson College Phonathon held its end-of-the-semester party. The Phonathon's student supervisors, including my coauthor Theresa, had asked their local burrito spot, Boloco, to cater the event, ordering 35 "inspired" burritos. However, when the supervisors arrived to pick up their order, they were informed that it wasn't ready—in fact, not a single one of their burritos had been wrapped. According to Boloco, the pickup time wasn't for hours. Confused over the miscommunication and anxious as the party's start time quickly approached, the four Emersonians did what any gen Yer would do in that situation: they tweeted about how annoyed they were with the wait. Normally, this isn't the most constructive thing to do, but Boloco is known for responding to complaints on Twitter; at the very least, the students figured they'd get an apology from the social media team (and maybe a few free burritos) in an hour or so. But that's not what happened. Three minutes after they tweeted their dissatis-faction, they received a response—from the CEO himself, John Pepper. First, Pepper apologized for the inconvenience, and then he gave them his cell phone number, asking the group to call him so he could sort things out. It was a Sunday and Pepper was at the gym, but that didn't matter to the CEO.

When the student supervisors hung up the phone, they dis-covered the cause of the missing burritos: their boss had acci-dentally submitted the wrong pickup time for the order. Theresa remembers how awful she and her fellow supervisors felt over the mistake, mortified that they had made such a fuss when Boloco wasn't in the wrong: "But the Boloco team told us not to worry and, recognizing the urgency of the situation, wrapped our burritos at record speed and delivered the order ahead of schedule and in time for the party." Pepper's accessibility and the staff's care and responsiveness had brightened an already sunny day for the Emerson College Phonathon.

Boloco, which stands for "Boston Local Company," is a regional chain offering "inspired" burritos and smoothies. Founded by CEO John Pepper in 1997, Boloco has expanded rap-idly throughout New England, and recently opened in the D.C. area. In addition to its creative menu, Boloco is known for its commitment to responding efficiently and effectively to each and every customer. On Twitter, this means that no tweet is left unanswered, and every mistake is apologized for and rectified with a free menu item. In the stores, this means that customers are given a voice in the creation of menu items.

Being thoroughly appreciative of feedback is the first step. The second is responding to it in a genuine way. At Boloco, staff members try to put themselves in their customers' shoes before responding, so that they can first empathize and understand where they're coming from. Responding defensively or coldly is worse than not responding at all. "People don't realize that when they forget to respond, while it may not seem like a big deal, it adds up," Pepper told me. He started responding just because he felt it was the right thing to do, but not knowing if it would even matter to his customers or business. At first, it didn't seem to, as people didn't reply, but Boloco now has developed a reputation for responding and creating open lines of communication between the company and customers.

Sure, negative feedback can sting. Pepper recalls a time when the company received a two-star review via Yelp from a first-time user. "Do you know what that means?" Pepper exclaims. "It means he created an account *just* to blast us!" It was heartbreaking. But that just reminded Pepper of how personal responsiveness is. People are hurt when they feel ignored and happy when they realize their voice matters. And at Boloco, it does: "Boloco is a result of the feedback of others over many, many years," says Pepper. Which is why he's the champion of responsiveness at the company.

On one occasion, Pepper was in New Hampshire and noticed a tweet from Boston complaining that the music at one of the Boloco locations was too loud. He immediately called the store, spoke with the manager, and told him, "Turn down the music. Just trust me." Pepper then wrote back to the disgruntled Boloco customer: "Done." It doesn't get more responsive than that.

RESPONDING EFFICIENTLY

Consumers are certainly not shy about sharing their opinions, and in today's age of digital communication and social media, they're more empowered than ever to make their voices heard. It's not enough to simply listen to your customers; you've got to let them know they're being heard by responding to them.

SavingStar, an electronic coupon company based in Waltham, Massachusetts, is known for its responsiveness. The team quickly answers posts and messages on its social media channels, addressing complaints and thanking customers for positive feedback. But SavingStar doesn't respond only via its own media, such as the brand's Facebook page or Twitter profile; instead, SavingStar seeks out conversations in other venues, such as blogs and forums, and addresses issues there as well.

Overwhelmingly, the customer response has been complete delight that the representatives would take the time to seek out channels other than their own and actually join the conversation. For instance, SavingStar recounted to me a time when it noticed multiple questions on weusecoupons.com. So the representatives created an account, jumped in, and answered the queries. Users were amazed and had an overwhelmingly positive response with exclamations such as "We didn't know that there was a rep on here! Pretty cool. Really great they're reading stuff about them and answering questions." SavingStar's responsiveness has created a loyal consumer base, which has led to many referrals and new customers. (See Figure 6.1.)

How quickly do you need to respond? The faster the better, of course. Generally, as soon as possible, whatever that means for your company and the resources you have available. But if it takes you more than 24 hours to get back to a customer, you should be trying harder. Build a model that allows you to respond at least "fast enough."

With the rise of social media, a great deal of customer complaints about products, services, or organizations have moved

Ann ▮▮▮▮ ▶ **SavingStar**
February 18 at 11:46pm · 🌐

Ugh, just checked my account and again I was not credited. This happened before and I never got my credit. This time though I purchased over $15 of Quaker products. The other items from that day credited. Kind of bummed I probably would not have purchased that much in one trip. Oh well guess I will be eating healthy for awhile.

Like · Comment

 SavingStar Hi Ann, We apologize for the inconvenience. Please email us the details of your purchase at support@savingstar.com so we can look into your account. We want to make sure you get your savings. Thanks, Josh
February 19 at 7:28am · Like

 SavingStar Please note only certain Quaker items were included in the promotion: Old Fashioned Quaker Oats, Instant Quaker Oatmeal, Oatmeal Squares, Grits & Whole Hearts
February 19 at 7:46am · Like

 Ann ▮▮▮▮ I will thank you. I bought 2 boxes of Instant Quaker Oatmeal, 1 box of Oatmeal Squares and 1 box of Whole Hearts.
February 19 at 4:38pm · Like

 SavingStar Hi Ann ▮▮▮▮ - It seems that the Quaker purchases are processed by our database a day or two behind the other purchases. They should appear in your account within 24-48 hours. Thanks! Josh
February 20 at 9:50am · Like

 Ann ▮▮▮▮ Good to know, thank you so much! You guys are awesome!!!
February 20 at 10:49am · Like

FIGURE 6.1   **SavingStar's responsiveness turns an angry customer into a loyal one.**
Source: SavingStar

with someone from our team, whether it's a top manager or an intern—insight into our business that has helped us launch new ideas, find and grow talent, and better understand our customers and opportunities.

As a social media CEO, responding to nonstaff is even more difficult than responding to staff. For obvious reasons, I choose to live a very public, active life in social media, with a robust presence on Facebook, Twitter, Instagram, foursquare, and a blog, among other channels. Since I preach the virtues of corporate responsiveness in social media, I figure the least I can do is respond to any and all questions and comments I get across social channels. Again, this has admittedly gotten more difficult as my social reach has grown (50,000+ Twitter followers these days), but answering people's questions has led to business opportunities and has helped me establish myself as a person who practices what he preaches. Plus, I figure if someone can keep a question to 140 characters or less, I can give an answer in 140 characters or less.

This commitment was put to the test in February 2012. I was leading a webinar (online seminar) for Media Bistro, teaching an introductory course on social media marketing to about 50 students. I closed the webinar the way I always close speeches, by suggesting to the students that if they had any questions, now or anytime, they should feel free to tweet me.

A week later I got an e-mail from a friend at seven in the morning that read, "Congrats on the *New York Times* coverage!"

"*Times* coverage?" I wondered. I didn't recall giving any recent interviews or announcing anything pressworthy. I scrambled to the *Times* website to look it up. As it turns out, unbeknownst to me, *New York Times* editor Jennifer Preston had been sitting in on the webinar for an article she was writing about social media education. Her article closed with the following:

> At the end of the first session, Mr. Kerpen from Likeable invited the students to find him on Twitter and ask any questions that they might have after the class. . . . He emphasized, "There is no timeline for tweeting me questions."
> "The timeline is the rest of our lives," he said.[9]

online. Social media amplifies every opinion, which can be a blessing or a curse depending on how great your product or organization is and how responsive your customer service teams are. With the conversation moving online, some organizations are moving their customer service teams online as well, allowing for speedy responses. Predictably, some are doing a considerably better job than others.

Take, for example, clothing retailer Old Navy. The clothing retailer produces a Twitter stream that's a powerhouse of customer service. Check the feed at any given time, and you'll find the company's responses to rave reviews ("Thanks! We're glad you like it!" says Old Navy), rants ("We're sorry this happened. Please e-mail us at custserv@oldnavy.com so we can fix this," says Old Navy), and customer questions ("The sale ends May 4," says Old Navy). Old Navy even has Twitter chats dedicated to making sure that its customers are happy and that their needs are being met.

Best Buy was the first large company to begin delivering unexpected value on Twitter in the form of answering people's questions. It developed the "Twelpforce," a group of nearly a thousand employees who were trained to respond to people's questions on Twitter about electronics products. When one of these hundreds of staff people isn't on the floor helping an in-person customer, he or she is helping online customers or prospects—and answering any questions about electronics products, including products not sold at Best Buy. Since sending the Twelpforce into action, Best Buy has received a number of customer service awards, including an Interactive Gold for Innovative Use of Technology at the 2010 Clio Awards.[1]

Depending on the size of your business, it might be next to impossible to respond to every single person. Responding efficiently and effectively takes proper prioritization. The customer who frequently reviews on Yelp or has 5,000 Twitter followers can cause far more damage to your business than a less vocal or less influential dissatisfied customer.

Many organizations are adopting instant messaging systems on their websites in order to address as many customer inquiries and problems as possible. Oklahoma State University's library system is an avid user of instant messaging for customer service. Students and faculty can message library staff to reserve conference rooms, inquire about the location or availability of materials, or get help with research. The system is convenient for patrons and library staff alike, and it allows the staff to do its job in a much more efficient manner. In this case, being responsive online is actually saving time.

There are many ways to build systems of responsiveness within your company. Some companies have developed an ecosystem within which others are able to help the company respond by building an extensive wiki-FAQs to ensure every question has an answer or by creating a place for consumers to speak to and aid each other, like the Apple fans who gather at the store's Genius Bar. Ask yourself what processes your company can put into place so that every phone call, e-mail, and customer is responded to promptly.

But remember: Responsiveness isn't something that matters only online. It's not just about responding to e-mails or blog comments. It means not putting your customer on hold for 25 minutes. It means sincerely taking customers' feedback into consideration.

CUSTOMERS HAVE A VOICE

When the makers of Necco Wafers changed their recipe to use natural flavoring in 2009, they thought they were making a change for the better. But their customers made it known, loud and clear, that this wasn't the case. The New England Confectionery Company's mail volume increased twenty-fold—some positive but mostly negative, with the most popular sentiment being "You ruined my product. I will never buy anything from you again." Whoops. As it turns out, customers weren't dissatisfied with the taste of the new product but the coloring. Learning of the strong sales of natural products, the New England Confectionary Company had changed a 162-year-old product in hopes of boosting Necco Wafers' flat sales. But the new colors didn't hold a familiar hue, and customers didn't recognize the product as the candy they had grown up with. In some of the feedback, customers included stories about their sentimental connection with the wafers: using them to practice for Communion or to serve as poker chips or to fool tollbooth machines. Once sales had dropped 35 percent, the company knew it had made a terrible mistake. So it took its customers' reactions to heart and returned to the artificial flavorings and original colors.[2]

Changes to your company's products or services needn't be fueled by the desire to earn more money. They can be fueled by making your customers happier.

RESPONSIVENESS DOESN'T HAVE TO BE ON TWITTER

Trader Joe's does not yet respond very well via digital channels. The specialty grocery store chain doesn't offer an e-mail for customers to contact and doesn't yet have a Facebook or Twitter account. But just about every Trader Joe's customer has a story about the company's responsiveness.

After one customer moved from Southern California to Reno, Nevada, she was disappointed to discover her new local Trader Joe's location didn't carry her beloved soy ice cream cookie. She was blown away by the swiftness with which the Reno Trader Joe's started stocking her favorite product after her request. Another customer was driving past her Phoenix Trader Joe's store early one morning when she found it busy before its official opening at 9 a.m. When she asked the manager what was going on, he responded, "A lot of people wanted us to be open early, so we try to be as often as we can."

Another loyal customer wrote a blog post about the time she went to her local Trader Joe's and was shocked to discover her favorite toothpaste wasn't on the shelf. When she asked a store "crew member" why, he replied that the store was no longer carrying the toothpaste because it wasn't selling very well. The customer was disappointed: where was she going to find her favorite nonminty, kid-friendly, fluoride-free toothpaste for $1.99? The employee was sympathetic and apologetic, but the customer had no choice except to buy a much more expensive, lackluster replacement. Soon after, however, she went back and—tada!—her toothpaste was back on the shelf, right where it belonged. She asked the cashier if she should stock up in anticipation of the toothpaste being pulled from the shelves again. The response: there had been such an outcry from customers that Trader Joe's decided to bring the toothpaste back for good. The customer, thoroughly delighted, declared that this had sealed her loyalty to Trader Joe's.[3]

At Trader Joe's, responding to customer feedback is about something very human: an open conversation between employees and customers. "We feel really close to our customers," vice president of marketing Audrey Dumper said. "When we want to know what's on their minds, we don't need to put them in a sterile room with a swinging lightbulb."

Store managers, or "captains," are given much autonomy to set up their stores to meet local needs and preferences. Each store employee can e-mail buyers directly with suggestions or customer feedback. The company's inventory itself is a response to customers' feedback: the company simply removes items that don't sell well to make room for new products. Says Dumper, "We like to think of Trader Joe's as an economic food democracy."[4]

Let your customers have a say in your company, and let them know their voices matter by reacting to their feedback.

GAP RESPONDS TO LOGO OUTRAGE IN THE NICK OF TIME

In early fall 2010, clothing retailer Gap was in the midst of a slump. Numbers had been down since the early 2000s, and Gap decided it was time to revamp its image. The way to go about this, Gap decided, would be to change the logo. Gap would go from its well-known "blue box" logo to a new logo that featured a smaller box above the *p*.

Gap's consumers were outraged by the change, and they flocked to social media to let the world know. A Twitter account set up to protest the change gained more than 5,000 followers, and Gap's Facebook page received more than 2,000 negative comments concerning the logo change. A "make your own Gap logo" site went viral, prompting close to 14,000 parody versions of the logo. Gap's Marka Hansen, president of Gap North America, decided enough was enough. Citing the outcry against the logo on social media, Hansen stated:

> We've been listening to and watching all of the comments this past week. We heard them say over and over again they are passionate about our blue box logo, and they want it back. So we've made the decision to do just that—we will bring it back across all channels. We've learned a lot in this process, and we are clear that we did not go about this in the right way. We recognize that we missed the opportunity to engage with the online community. This wasn't the right project at the right time for crowd-sourcing. There may be a time to evolve our logo, but if and when that time comes, we'll handle it in a different way.[5]

The logo gaffe cost Gap a $247 million stock drop.[6] Rather than ignoring the public outcry about the logo and carrying on, Gap elected to respond to consumers and make a change. The outrage resulting from the initial logo change could have escalated, become more of a disaster, and cost Gap even more sales, but instead the debacle proved to be a valuable learning experience for Gap about the value of using social media to connect with consumers. Gap was able to see that its customers were unhappy with the change, respond to the issue, and maintain a positive relationship with its best customers. The company's stock responded positively as well, immediately rising after the original logo returned.[7]

JETBLUE'S B6 BLACK OPS

The customer service team members at JetBlue are firm believers in the importance of being responsive. Their goal is to bring humanity back to air travel, and they know that there's nothing more human than conversation and engagement. JetBlue's customer service team is well aware that the ability to listen and respond to communities represents a great opportunity to improve business and make sure customers invest in the business.

One of JetBlue's customer service priorities is speed. Send a frantic tweet to JetBlue about a lost bag or a missed flight, and you can expect a response within 15 minutes, 24 hours a day, 7 days a week. The members of the team at JetBlue don't limit their quick response strategy to their own pages. Instead, they listen to conversations on multiple channels, jumping in when necessary to clarify an inaccurate statement or to join witty banter among customers.

The team that handles the online responses is called the "Real-Time Recovery Team," nicknamed "B6 Black Ops." B6 Black Ops is responsible for answering e-mails, talking to customers with special needs, and monitoring social media channels. The 20-person team works 24/7 to ensure that everything is running smoothly. The team members are able to help out not only with common questions but with in-depth information about the airline that customers need to know, like whether or not the windows on the planes are UV protected.

B6 Black Ops tries to reach out to everyone, which can sometimes mean extending the two-person shift to an all-hands-on-deck situation, particularly in instances of inclement weather, like when Hurricane Irene hit during the summer of 2011. In such cases, the Real-Time Recovery Team is more efficient at handling customer concerns over Twitter than it is via other channels, such as telephone customer service lines. (See Figure 6.2.) The team was actually able to reschedule flights via Twitter when the phone lines were jammed.

JetBlue's biggest strength might be the total reach of the company's policy of responsiveness, which extends far beyond social media. In one instance, a JetBlue customer at JFK was traveling with a small folding bicycle in a checked bag. When the customer arrived at the baggage-drop counter, he was dismayed to discover that JetBlue charges an extra fee for transporting bicy-

FIGURE 6.2   **The "wing walls" of JetBlue's Long Island City Support Center show a Twitter search feed to ensure responsiveness.**
Source: Morgan Johnston, JetBlue

cles, even though his bicycle was neatly folded into his carry-on bag and clearly was not taking up any extra space. The customer tweeted about the incident, which led the Real-Time Recovery Team to do a bit of digging. As a result of the ordeal, not only did the customer receive a refund for the extra charges, but JetBlue ended up altering its policy on bicycles.

BEING ACCESSIBLE

Kat Cole is the president of Cinnabon, Inc., an American baked-goods store known for its massive cinnamon rolls. Take a stroll around your local airport or shopping mall, and you're fairly likely to find one—they're everywhere. Kat Cole is too. She travels around the country attending conferences and meetings and visiting store locations to say hello to bakers and see how everything's going. Cole is constantly busy, but she always finds time for the things that are important to her. One of the things that are most important to Cole is engaging with her customers. Send a tweet to @Cinnabon, and you'll not only get a reply from Cinnabon but a tweet from Cole as well. She thanks her customers for kind words, urges them to petition for a Cinnabon location in their hometown, and engages them in witty banter. Cole could easily sit back and let the Cinnabon social media team do the work of engaging customers, but instead she gets involved. That extra engagement of the CEO and the accessibility to her humanize the Cinnabon brand by showing customers that everyone from the top down truly cares about their satisfaction.

Being accessible allows you to be responsive. Most companies are not so large that their leaders can't devote time to hearing about what's going on with the staff and learning what they can do better. A likeable leader is accessible to his or her team. Accessibility allows a company to be responsive to customers as well. Karmaloop founder and CEO Greg Selkoe even lists his e-mail address and cell phone directly on his company's website. The practice started organically; when customers bought something from the site, he would call them and ask how they heard of Karmaloop, an online retailer specializing in men's and women's streetwear. Now, it's a philosophy he advocates: "I think if you stand behind your product, you should be accessible."[8] At a likeable company, anyone can reach out to anyone else and expect a response.

RESPONSIVENESS ISN'T ALWAYS EASY—BUT IT IS WORTH IT

As an entrepreneur in social media, I've been a firm believer in the value of personal responsiveness for years. I make it a point to respond to each and every e-mail I get from our 100+ staff and interns, and I agree to spend 15 minutes with any employee or intern who wants time with me. Sure, this policy has gotten a lot harder to maintain as we've grown quickly in the past few years; and eventually the 15 minutes might have to become 5 minutes, and some e-mails may take longer to return. But I firmly plan on holding to this policy. I gain valuable insight each time I talk

I ended up getting over 900 questions via Twitter that day, and, of course, I had to answer each and every one. I didn't know whether to laugh or cry about the free publicity. A few weeks later, however, I met the editor at the *Times* who had written the story, and we shared a laugh over it. As it turned out, my bold declaration and time spent answering 900 tweets were definitely worth the relationship I was able to establish with an editor at arguably the most important publication around.

Feel free to put me to the test right now (or anytime for the rest of your life): tweet me a question at Twitter.com/DaveKerpen. I'd be flattered you took the time and thought to ask, and I'll be as responsive as humanly possible.

THE RETURNS ON YOUR REPLIES

Jimmy John's is a sandwich delivery chain in the southwestern United States that promises "freaky fast" service. The Jimmy John's team members have a fun, lighthearted attitude that is evident from the sandwich makers to the corporate office to social media. Whether you tweet at Jimmy John's or visit one of the restaurants in person, you'll get a "How's it goin', man" or "Hey, bro!" When it comes to conveying its company culture in social media channels, Jimmy John's has it down. Aside from the fact that the Jimmy John's team members sound a little like surfers, they have a strong set of values in place from the top down, online and off. They believe in delivering value along with their sandwiches and doing everything possible to ensure that their customers have a positive experience every time they visit Jimmy John's. The website asks, "Good experience? Bad experience? We want to know." If customers are continually having bad experiences, Jimmy John's evaluates the problem and fixes it—simple as that.

As a popular brand that's active on social media, Jimmy John's receives a lot of tweets and Facebook posts. Good or bad, it responds. However, Jimmy John's goes a step further than the usual "We're sorry to hear that" or "Thanks." If there's a problem, Jimmy John's team members work to fix it. There's not always an immediate solution, but there's always a happier (or at least less angry) customer. And if a customer sends Jimmy John's a tweet full of praise, the team not only says thanks but retweets the tweet to share with all its followers. Jimmy John's neutralizes the negative opinions and amplifies the positive ones. And it pays off—Jimmy John's is now well known for its stellar customer service online and off and pulls in more than $1.2 million a year.

Essentially, the business value of responsiveness is the neutralization of unhappy customers in order to retain their business coupled with the amplification of happy customers to increase business. Respond to the haters, and you'll turn them into lovers. Respond to the lovers, and you'll multiply the love.

THE FOUR MOST IMPORTANT WORDS IN BUSINESS

The four most important words in business are "I'm sorry" and "Thank you." It's amazing how powerful "I'm sorry" is in business and, for that matter, in life. "I'm sorry" lets people know that you hear them, that you care, and that you feel bad. When someone says "I'm sorry" to you and validates how you feel, as a customer you're likely to feel better, no matter how angry you might have felt prior to the apology. While corporate lawyers aren't always fans of putting "I'm sorry" in writing, it really does go a long way toward defusing problems. Take a look at the screenshot in Figure 6.3. You can see from the messages that Taylor posted on the Entenmann's

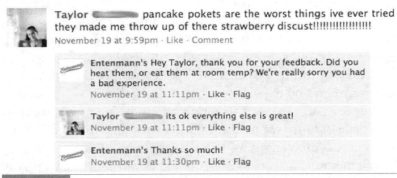

Taylor ⬛⬛⬛ pancake pokets are the worst things ive ever tried they made me throw up of there strawberry discust!!!!!!!!!!!!!!!!!!!!
November 19 at 9:59pm · Like · Comment

Entenmann's Hey Taylor, thank you for your feedback. Did you heat them, or eat them at room temp? We're really sorry you had a bad experience.
November 19 at 11:11pm · Like · Flag

Taylor ⬛⬛⬛ its ok everything else is great!
November 19 at 11:11pm · Like · Flag

Entenmann's Thanks so much!
November 19 at 11:30pm · Like · Flag

FIGURE 6.3 **Saying sorry goes a long way toward quickly fixing a problem.**

Facebook page, she quickly went from being angry to reminding herself and the world how much she loved Entenmann's other products—all basically because of those two big words.

If "I'm sorry" is powerful in defusing customer anger, "Thank you" is even more important to validate the positive feelings your customers have. We'll talk more about gratitude in Chapter 11, but the idea is that those two simple words, again, let people know that you hear them, that you care, and that you appreciate them. They say that every happy customer is worth responding to, not just unsatisfied ones. "Thank you," whether spoken in person, on the phone, or through social media, tells people that they matter and motivates them to continue to spread the word about you to their friends.

THE RAMIFICATIONS OF BEING SILENT

The ramifications of not responding to one customer? You lose one customer. The ramifications of not responding to lots of customers? You lose lots of customers.

Things are going to go wrong; that's the nature of the universe. The problem isn't when something goes wrong; it's when something goes wrong and a business does nothing about it, no response and no rectification. When you don't respond, you're sending a message that you simply don't care about your customers. And they hear that message loud and clear.

Responsiveness means not putting a customer on hold for 25 minutes. Responsiveness means staffing appropriately so that you have the resources to respond to everyone. When you call a big company and get the "unusually high call volume" message, what do you think? "Yeah right!" That's simply not possible: a company can't be experiencing an unusually high call volume all the time; otherwise, it wouldn't be "unusual," would it? How about when you're on hold for 45 minutes and you hear, "Your call is very important to us"? Um, doesn't seem like it!

When your customers are being shut out by your company and a competitor lends an ear and gives an appreciative response, where do you think your customers will be doing business from now on? People won't tolerate being disrespected and having their time wasted. There will come a breaking point where you will lose them forever. Remember, not responding is a response. It's a response that says, "We don't care."

BANK OF AMERICA INDUCES TEARS

One of my book research team members, Val, recently had what she describes as the worst customer service experience of her life. Val moved to New York City in January 2012 in order to join our team. She's from Texas, and so the move was a big one. After sorting out the important, need-to-know things about New York City life—such as which trains to take and who sells the best bagels—Val decided it was time to open a new bank account. "My old bank only has locations in the southwestern U.S., so I thought it might make things a little inconvenient," Val told me. "Of course, I now know a whole new meaning of 'inconvenient'!"

Val decided to set up her account with Bank of America. There's a location very close to Likeable's New York City office, and so she figured it wouldn't be a problem for her to go to the branch if need be. "When I set up my account, everything was fine," she said. "I waited for about 10 minutes when I got in, but they gave me a temporary card that I was able to use that day. It was only after I deposited my first paycheck that things took a turn for the worse." Val explained that when she deposited her check, the receipt stated that she would have a portion of the funds immediately available. She decided to use those funds to go ahead and pay her rent a little early to get it out of the way. However, when she checked the next morning, her account was overdrawn. Confused, Val decided to use the customer service instant messaging system on the Bank of America website. But the website, three customer-service-line associates, and two in-person visits to the bank proved unhelpful.

On the day her check was supposed to clear, it didn't. She'd had enough, and so she turned to social media. She tweeted, "Worst customer service EVER award goes to @BofA_Help" and asked her friends and followers to retweet. A few of them came through, and Bank of America's social media team was bombarded with tweets about how much they stink.

"I imagine they get that a lot," Val said. "They tweeted me back, offering to help me. Surprising, considering how unhelpful the rest of their customer service team was."

The next morning, the money was there, but the damage had already been done. Val closed her account. She also wanted to make sure that her friends, her followers, and their followers never had to go through what she went through. She wrote two blog posts, several statuses on Facebook, and, of course, a tweet that bounced around through her friend circle, all with the goal of making sure no one else had to deal with Bank of America and its awful customer service.

There's an old saying that if someone has a good experience, he or she will tell 1 friend, but if a person has a bad experience, he or she will tell 5. In today's digital world, that 5 becomes 500 or even 5,000. Bank of America lost 1 customer when it lost Val, but it lost 100 more when she told her story.

RESPONSIVENESS: SOCIAL TOOLS AND PRINCIPLES

Remember the comment cards that companies used to have for customers to submit their compliments and complaints? Today's version of comment cards is social media, soliciting feedback from consumers. It may seem daunting to you as a business; in the past you may have tried to control your public image, and now anyone can potentially ruin your reputation with a single tweet. You might be tempted to ignore the negative comments you receive or even delete them, but ignoring a customer on social media is like putting him or her on hold and never getting back on the line. It's like hanging up the phone on your customers—only worse, because millions of people are watching. And deleting a comment or post or review is like ripping up a comment card in a customer's face. Once you begin to accept and even embrace the possibility of negative feedback, you can begin to formulate a plan to respond to all of it.

Speed of response on social networks is always challenging. Put yourself in your customer's shoes: if you complained on Facebook, Twitter, or Yelp about an experience, would you want a response in the next week or the next hour? The truth is, the sooner you respond to customers, the better. That said, your ability and need to respond quickly will depend on your industry and your resources. If you're an art dealer, you probably don't need to respond to a Facebook post in the middle of the night. If you're an airline, however, you likely do. In general, the longer you go without responding, the worse off you'll be. But it's never too late to show your customers—and more importantly, the world that's watching—that you care.

Social media is the great equalizer of our time, giving everyone a voice. Companies have no choice today but to listen and to respond. The likeable company is one that systematically responds to every empowered customer.

ACTION ITEMS

1. Develop a system to take feedback into consideration and allow your customers to have a say in your company.
2. Write a list of five ways you can respond to negative feedback and constructively use it to improve your business.
3. Take inventory of your available resources and your system for responding efficiently across a wide variety of communication channels: Facebook, Twitter, e-mail, telephone, and, yes, even snail mail.

LISTENING HELPS ONLY WHEN YOU RESPOND AS WELL

It may not seem like it, but you're saying a lot when you say nothing at all. Ignoring a problem won't make it go away. You can't place your hands over your ears and say, "I can't hear you!" and expect things to get better. Sure, the negative feedback might eventually let up, but you won't have solved anything or taken advantage of an opportunity to convert an outraged customer into a satisfied, loyal one. Respond to your colleagues' and customers' feedback—whether on social networks, online, on the phone, or in person—and let them know they have a valued voice.

CHAPTER 7

Adaptability
Change or Perish

When you're finished changing, you're finished.

—Ben Franklin

When you walk into the office of Ford's CEO Alan Mulally, your eyes are immediately drawn to the reproduction of a *Saturday Evening Post* spread hanging on his wall. The watercolor image (shown in Figure 7.1) depicts a young family looking at a line of cars with the Ford factory in the background. The picture is accompanied by the tagline "Opening the highways to all mankind." That was Henry Ford's mission: to make transportation affordable to every person who wanted it. After nearly a century of business, Ford is still in line with this original vision.

Of course, the execution of the vision has changed a lot; today, it means affordable fuel efficiency and in-car technology for all. In 2006, the company had to take stock of where it was in the industry and be very honest with itself. Alan made the bold decision to mortgage everything Ford had, getting a loan of $23 billion to pour into the product development department. He knew that in order to succeed, the company had to make cars that were top of the line with fuel efficiency, and he was ruth-

FIGURE 7.1 **Ford has never lost sight of its original vision.**
Source: Scott Monty

lessly determined to do whatever it took. Ford's ability to adapt its vision in consideration of the current marketplace and consumer demand, no matter the risk, ultimately saved the company from a bailout and earned a $2.7 billion profit.

Twenty years ago, the introduction of the Ford Explorer established the SUV category. In 2010, the company reinvented the iconic vehicle, transforming its design and capabilities.

Scott Monty, global head of social media at Ford, told me, "Because we had reinvented the vehicle, we knew we had to reinvent the way we presented it to the public."

In the past, cars were unveiled at auto shows, but Ford decided to unveil the new Ford Explorer in eight cities simultaneously and on Facebook, giving fans exclusive advance notice. All communications efforts, from broadcast media to digital integration, were focused on the launch. On July 26, 2010, Ford finally unveiled the Explorer with a combination of earned, owned, and paid media, creating incredible results. Ford was able to reach 99 million people on social media and 400 million online, with 500,000 home-page visits as opposed to the normal 10,000. The company calculated its marketing efforts had greater impact that day than if it had bought a Super Bowl ad. The Ford Explorer was the number one trending topic on Twitter and number two trend on Google, ousted only by Lindsay Lohan due to her recent stay at a rehabilitation center.

Ford was the first automaker to reveal a vehicle via Facebook, and for its ability to adapt to changing market conditions, the company reaped much better results than it would have with a traditional auto show press launch: sales went up 100 percent from the previous year. "It's easy to be myopic," says Scott, "and live within the industry bubble." But if you look outside your industry, you will be able to react to changing consumer behavior with strong results. With innovative technology that adapts to the road ahead, the redesigned Explorer is the epitome of adaptability. The same can be said of Ford.

Although Ford has 200,000 employees, the company has structured itself to remain open to change. Each member of the team carries around a card with the four-point Ford mantra, which includes the strategy to "aggressively restructure" in the face of the changing marketplace. In order for Ford to remain an innovative company, its employees must have a willingness to be courageous and open to change. As the original tinkerer, Henry Ford instilled into the DNA of the company a drive to innovate and adapt, and that spirit is still alive in each Ford team member today.

ADAPTING TO YOUR CUSTOMERS

The larger your company is, the more difficult it may be to adapt. The good news is, chances are, your company isn't as large as Ford. And even if it is, here's another example of a huge company that's learned how to adapt.

Walmart was built on the promise of delivering the best prices to consumers. However, in recent years, as the price gap between the retail giant and rivals has drastically narrowed, the company knows it needs a new breakthrough. It's looking to Walmart Labs to find it.

Although Walmart is the biggest retailer in the world, it's not the biggest player in e-commerce—that's Amazon. Walmart knew it needed to understand changing consumer behavior and the digital marketplace. Walmart Labs was formed to ensure that Walmart is at the forefront of e-commerce 2.0 so that the company can help define the future of retail rather than play catch-up.

The Walmart Labs initiative is responsible for Walmart's April 2011 purchase of Kosmix, a tech start-up that had previously created Junglee for Amazon, which then became the Amazon Marketplace of third-party vendors who drive a large percentage of e-commerce sales. Smaller ideas and projects specific to e-commerce, as well as long-term social media strategies, have emerged, pushing Walmart to innovate and stay on top of consumer trends. Walmart Labs has allowed the retail giant to improve the product recommendations on Walmart.com, tap into shoppers' smartphones as a marketing channel, and listen to social media conversations in the vicinity of specific physical locations to determine what products each store should stock.

In 2011, Walmart's online shopping growth far exceeded the industry average. The company recognized the importance of keeping up with a constantly changing environment and, in adapting, has been able to conquer the threat to its dominance, tech-savvy bargain shoppers.

An adaptable company is able to meet the ever-changing needs of its customers. Your customers aren't stagnant; your business can't be either. In a dynamic environment, you can't expect to stand still or stubbornly hold to your company's product or service offerings. Without being open to new demands from consumers, you will be losing out not only on the opportunity to improve your business, but on potential customers and sales.

ENDLESS ADAPTABILITY

Will Curran, owner and president of Endless Entertainment, a teen entertainment company, goes out of his way to satisfy his clients, even if their requests exceed the "typical." Endless Entertainment offers customized, rather than "cookie-cutter," packages, with the philosophy that each person is different, and so should each event be. Granted, most event-planning companies will do a consultation for their customers. What really sets Will and his team at Endless Entertainment apart is their willingness to try just about anything. For example, he told me that, on one occasion, the company was putting together the entertainment for a high school prom. Will went through each service he could provide, and then the client asked, "Can we have live tigers?" Will didn't miss a beat: "Absolutely." If he doesn't have the specific equipment a client needs, he goes out and buys it just for that one event. When the Endless Entertainment team hosted a New Year's bash sponsored by the Tostitos Fiesta Bowl, the team created a chip-shaped mirror ball that "dipped" into the crowd. Was this on Will's list of services? Of course not, but that didn't stop him from rising to the challenge and expanding his company's capabilities. "Don't think outside the box," says Will. "Crush the box."

And Endless Entertainment has crushed expectations. Will's unyielding desire to find solutions for his customers has gained Endless Entertainment recognition from *Inc.* magazine as the "Coolest College Startup" and earned him acceptance into the Entrepreneurs' Organization's prestigious Accelerator program, designed to bring businesses from $250,000 in revenue to $1 million in three years.

MAKE PIVOTS

Making a change in your company does not require completely refocusing your vision or abandoning your original mission. In fact, adaptability involves just the opposite: not a completely new path or a gigantic leap, but simply a pivot.

In *The Lean Startup*, Eric Ries describes pivoting as the ability to change direction while staying grounded in a particular vision. As opposed to ridiculously risky jumps in strategy, pivots leverage valuable previous learning. Had Twitter not pivoted, it would still be a podcasting service, rather than a huge microblogging success.[1] Fab.com pivoted and was reborn from the ashes of a failed gay social network called Fabulis.

Business leaders who learn how to pivot "keep one foot in the past, and place one foot in a new possible future." Forty years ago, Richard Branson published an indie music magazine, and Virgin Records was a small record store with just one location. The Marriott Corporation began as a root beer stand in Washington, D.C.[2] There's no business crystal ball; you have to be willing and able to take external forces of change as they come and pivot accordingly.

Mark Pincus, founder of Zynga, has been called a "serial entrepreneur." But that's only because, as he says, before Zynga, he failed to create a sustainable company. His slew of failures taught him a valuable lesson that he brought to Zynga: "Fail fast, look at the data, and move on."[3] While his vision never changes, he makes constant pivots in strategy until he finds one that works. And clearly he has, as he built a sustainable, $1.2 billion company[4] with 54 million active daily users[5] accounting for 126 percent[6] of Facebook's revenue. Of course, with Zynga's devastating stock dive in the summer of 2012, it may be time for another pivot.

Adaptability requires a build-measure-learn feedback loop within your company. This allows your business to achieve an overall vision in small increments, constantly pivoting as you go. You build your product or service, you measure results, and you learn from your mistakes or successes. Build, measure, learn, repeat—always pivoting.

THEKBUZZ ADAPTS TO BECOME LIKEABLE; THE ONLY CONSTANT IS CHANGE

When we started our company, theKbuzz, five years ago following our wedding, we were focused on word-of-mouth and buzz marketing. We did guerilla (face-to-face) marketing for clients, including mall events, store grand openings, and, yes, even more baseball stadium promotions. Late in our first year, 2007, we were fortunate to land a huge client in Verizon—organizing, hosting, and promoting house parties for its FiOS television, Internet, and phone package in a program we named Fans of FiOS. The idea was to find happy FiOS customers who would invite all their friends and neighbors over to their houses to watch a big TV event, thereby spreading the word about FiOS service and generating leads for new customers.

The program went well, but one of our biggest challenges was recruiting existing customers to host parties. We expected it would be easy—who wouldn't want to have a big party at his or her house paid for by someone else? But it turned out to be really difficult to find FiOS customers in many of the target areas, as it was a relatively new service with low penetration. In search of FiOS customers, we turned to Facebook, a social network my college intern told me about that had recently opened up beyond college students.

We started a Fans of FiOS Facebook page and began using Facebook advertisements to target people to recruit them for house parties. The page grew to 10,000 people in a few months, and we not only found party hosts, but also found a new business model. Word-of-mouth marketing could happen much more efficiently through Facebook and other social networks than through face-to-face marketing. So we began developing Facebook pages, apps, and campaigns for our clients and slowed down the cumbersome and less effective mall and stadium and store events. Online work was much more scalable as well, and we were able to grow theKbuzz 4,000 percent from 2007 to 2010.

In 2010, several weeks before the launch of the like button for Facebook pages, we adapted once again. As social media had emerged, we realized it was about so much more than creating buzz and word-of-mouth marketing. It was about customer service, sales, reputation management, and public relations. Social media, as we saw it, was about creating organizations, ones that listened to customers and were responsive and transparent in their interactions. Social media was about creating more likeable organizations. So we changed our name from theKbuzz to Likeable Media and broadened our focus to include consulting, training, and service areas outside marketing. Equally important, we also changed our mission from "creating and sustaining buzz for our clients" to "creating a more likeable world." The Likeable brand was a much stronger brand name than theKbuzz, and the company continued its rapid growth in 2010 and 2011.

In 2012, we adapted once again, adding the Likeable Local Facebook marketing product for small business. For years, we had struggled with how to properly service needy small businesses and still make a profit. Small businesses had the same needs as our large-brand clients, but obviously way fewer resources and smaller budgets. We realized in order to best serve them, we needed a technology-based platform with services to support it, rather than a straight service offering. Likeable Local was born and will, we hope, help Likeable continue to grow as a company. We even added "adaptability" as one of our company's core values, as we realized the only constant in the world was change, and we all wanted not only to keep up but to be ahead of the quickly changing times.

BUILDING A NIMBLE COMPANY

For your business to accept new opportunities and react to change, it must be inherently nimble. This takes a leader who is able to bend his or her goals or strategies based on results and opportunities. If you remain open to alternatives, listen, analyze, and brace yourself to react, you can adjust on the fly and take advantage of new possibilities.

To accommodate and execute change, a company must be flat, rather than hierarchical, in structure. An excess of management and direct reports slows down the process of change and deters new, possibly brilliant ideas from coming to fruition. Every member of your company should be able to deploy a great idea. A flat organization also better serves the needs of its customers; you should be able and willing to move employees around based on what's needed. By being nimble, you automatically set yourself up for success, no matter what curveballs the future throws your way.

Wildfire Interactive started in 2008 by providing an easy way for companies to run Facebook sweepstakes. Founders Victoria Ransom and Alain Chuard had owned a travel company that had a Facebook page. Wanting to attract fans, Ransom decided to give away a trip via a sweepstakes. However, due to

Facebook's strict contesting rules, Victoria and Alain needed to use a third-party application in order to run the sweepstakes. So they built one themselves. And when they noticed other companies, including Zappos and Kayak, wanting to use what they had created, they decided to start Wildfire, quickly expanding their software beyond Facebook, making it easy for businesses to run social media marketing campaigns via various channels.

They soon realized that they were addressing only one element of the social media marketing mix—how to build a community through promotions—and that companies wanted one platform to solve all solutions, rather than using many different vendors. So Wildfire chose to adapt again, focusing its developer resources on an advanced platform. The company was able to dramatically evolve its product offerings without having to change its vision at all: at the end of the day, the focus was still to create software that is scalable, intuitive, and easy to use, while helping clients get and measure results. Evolving the product was a gamble, but it paid off; as Wildfire moved toward a fast prescription model, it was able to attract far more customers.

Wildfire pivots, changing strategy without changing vision. As it seeks to meet the needs of the market, it never loses focus. The nimbleness of the company allows for these quick pivots. When Facebook changed from FBML to iframe, Wildfire decided to take advantage of the change by offering an easy way for companies to use iframes. The company had one week to get it done, timed it perfectly with Facebook's announcement, and received both media coverage and millions of users.

How does Wildfire do it? How does it manage to react so quickly to new opportunities and willingly take risks? It's part of the company's culture.

To keep up with and anticipate constant changes in the industry, Wildfire employs agile software development: every two weeks, Wildfire deploys new technology for its products, each time reevaluating the company's road map. These changes are driven by customers. By listening to the sales team, the company is able to understand what customers want right now and then quickly refocus developer resources in order to implement those changes.

Wildfire makes a point of hiring people who like change and are unafraid to take risks. These are people who are driven by passion and have done a lot with their lives. Employees don't take themselves too seriously and never get too comfortable. Victoria and Alain have deployed a team that challenges them and takes the company in new directions.

As the company has grown, layers of management have been added, with more people to loop in on decisions and projects, making change more challenging but certainly not impossible. Wildfire remains nimble; with a flat organizational structure, all employees are encouraged to speak up and are trusted and empowered to make decisions—there's no bureaucracy holding up a great, revolutionary idea. And Wildfire's ability to adapt was rewarded in July 2012 with its acquisition by Google for over $250 million.

IN FAST-MOVING TIMES, IT'S MORE IMPORTANT TO BE FLEXIBLE

In 1993, Pippa and Ron Seichrist created a professional ad school in Miami. The mission of the Miami Ad School was to be a collaboration between education and industry, giving students the best training possible, serving as a bridge between wanting a job in advertising and having one. The Seichrists created a curriculum that was hands-on, with realistic assignments. Instructors were working industry professionals, including Alex Bogusky of the Crispin Porter agency.

Yet as great as the top talent of Miami was, Pippa and Ron knew they needed additional points of view, and so they began recruiting industry professionals from all over the world. This new initiative was dubbed the Industry Hero Series, with each art director, copywriter, or planner donning a mask and cape as he or she worked on briefs with the students. The cross-pollination and diversity of ideas had an incredible impact on the school, producing award-winning graduates, most of whom left the school with multiple job offers. (See Figure 7.2.)

FIGURE 7.2   **The Miami Ad School has stayed nimble in order to provide an optimal experience for its students.**
Source: Pippa Seichrist

With the success of the school, Pippa and Ron could have stopped there, but they had an idea: Why don't we start doing the opposite? Instead of just bringing great thinkers to our students, why not send our students to great thinkers?

This one adventurous thought led to an era of change and growth for the school. The Quarter Away program was launched, allowing students to easily move from city to city. The program began with the creation of a new campus in booming Minneapolis. Hearing of the school's success, Leo Burnett of Chicago asked if the Quarter Away program could be extended with yearlong internships at the agency. This was something new for Miami Ad School, but the fact that it wasn't in line with the school's formula didn't stop Ron and Pippa from taking advantage of the opportunity. From there, the school rapidly expanded to New York and then globally, beginning with London. Lee Daley, who had recently taken the helm at Saatchi and Saatchi, made an overseas phone call to Pippa and Ron on Thanksgiving to ask if they could get a Miami Ad School up and running at his agency in London by the beginning of January. This would give them just over a month, including the holidays, to recruit students and move them to London. The school launched on time, and Lee personally greeted students the first morning they walked through the agency's doors.

Soon after, Fred Goldberg at Goldberg Moser O'Neil in San Francisco made a similar call to Ron and Pippa. "We hear you want to start a school in San Francisco," he said, "but you can't afford the high rents here. So I want you to start your school in our new agency building. And the space is free to you. I want you to be my legacy." Six months later, another call came from Oliver Joss, the COO at Jung von Matt in Hamburg. Then came Madrid, followed by São Paulo, Buenos Aires, Istanbul, Sydney, Berlin, Moscow, Beijing, Paris, Mumbai, Brussels, and Stockholm.

With the start of each new location, a roadblock emerged—students' perceptions, accreditation, housing, expenses, timing—but because Ron and Pippa refused to be formulaic and were open to any and all solutions, Miami Ad School became a global network with over 20 locations filled with unbelievable educational opportunities for its students.

Each change offered more possibilities. When they couldn't bring a Miami Ad School to Lagos, Nigeria, Ron and Pippa decided to teach the entire creative department of DDB Lagos via Skype from the Berlin school since the two locations had similar time zones. Other agencies soon asked for specialized training for their staff as well, and thus the Miami Ad School Pro program was born, offering tailor-made classes for agency and client staffers.

Ron and Pippa took a flexible view of education. "School" didn't have to be a single building where students go to learn. School could be a collection of cultural and professional experiences. Students at Miami Ad School can customize their own educations. No two students have the same career path, and in this industry, where change is the only constant, a flexible education has been the key to the school's success.

There's one thing the school is not willing to change, though. When Ron and Pippa first started Miami Ad School, they had a chocolate Labrador retriever named Fudge. Fudge was Ron's inseparable companion for nine years before being diagnosed with an inoperable brain tumor. The Lab's passing was devastating not only to Ron and Pippa, but to the school's students, staff, instructors, grads, and board members. Ron and Pippa received over 200 condolence e-mails and cards. In one, a student recalled a time he was called to Ron's office; he worried he was in trouble, but he calmed down when Fudge jumped up and sat with him on the sofa. A couple of months later, the students, staff, instructors, grads, and board members of Miami Ad School gave Ron and Pippa a chocolate Labrador retriever puppy. With the puppy, who was named Smudge, they presented a card noting their sentiment that Miami Ad School just wasn't the same without a chocolate Lab. Now, every campus has its own chocolate Lab. In fact, there's a line item in each contract that states, "Must have a dog." And Pippa and Ron are not willing to be flexible on that point.

THE McSWEENEY'S MANTRA

McSweeney's, founded in 1998 by author and editor Dave Eggers, is a small but notable publishing house in San Francisco. Originally launched as a magazine featuring only work that had been previously rejected by other magazines, McSweeney's expanded, publishing quarterly literary, food, sports, and DVD journals, a monthly magazine, a daily literary and humor website, and two additional imprints, Believer Books and Collins Library. Traditional publishing companies typically have far greater resources, but even with just 10 full-time employees, McSweeney's has been significantly more innovative than traditional houses, all thanks to its nimbleness and willingness to take risks.

The publisher's mantra, according to managing editor Eli Horowitz, is "Never having done something before is a bad reason not to do it."[7] According to Eli, the company has frequently decided to do things it's not technically qualified to do and doesn't have the resources for. This risk-taking mentality has earned McSweeney's a number of prestigious literary and design awards, as well as record sales. The publisher was even able to fully embrace the digital age by launching its own iPhone and iPad app. Beyond being praised for its design and user experience, the app experienced exceptional results: within three hours of the launch, the app surged to the top of the U.S. iTunes book category, broke the top 50 in the overall highest-grossing list, and created a great deal of word-of-mouth publicity via Twitter. This was a technological leap of faith, but it paid off, all because McSweeney's was unafraid to do things it didn't necessarily know how to do.

The lesson here? Don't fear change; fear *not* changing. Even if you've never done something before, do it. Even if you've never gone down a particular path, blaze it.

WHAT HAPPENS WHEN YOU DON'T ADAPT?

Business success is Darwinism at its finest. Just as in human evolution, survival of the fittest will determine the ultimate success or failure of your business. Circuit City and Borders are examples of companies that didn't survive, being paralyzed with fear in the face of changing consumer behavior and the digital age.

Circuit City was founded in 1949 and enjoyed great success. In fact, author Jim Collins referred to it as a "Good to Great company" in his 2001 classic, *Good to Great*. In 1992, the value of $1 in Circuit City stock was $311.64. Unfortunately, Circuit City couldn't keep up with the rapidly changing times. The company was complacent, a clear mistake in the aggressively competitive and fast-moving electronics industry. By deciding not to move into gaming as other retailers did, and not to do large in-store promotions with successful companies such as Apple, Circuit City created an opening for Best Buy, now the top electronics retailer in the United States. Circuit City also failed to improve its online presence, just as online retailers such as Amazon were starting to really take off. The once number two electronics retailer in the United States filed for bankruptcy in November 2008 and closed all 567 of its stores in January 2009.

Borders's big mistake was sticking too stubbornly to its retail presence, investing money to improve the in-store experience for customers and expanding globally. The company invested heavily in physical stores as consumers were flocking to the Internet. Borders treated the Internet like a passing trend, outsourcing online operations to Amazon until it finally decided to take control in 2008. But by then it was too late: the retailer was already in debt, lagging behind, and short on cash to invest. The deal with Amazon was ultimately a win for the online retailer: by the time Borders debuted its own website, Amazon had taken a massive portion of the online market share. Borders was always one step behind, going heavily into CD and DVD sales just as the industry was going digital. The company waited far too long to get into e-readers and e-books, and once it did, it was too broke to spend enough on devising a digital strategy. Again, Borders outsourced the problem, this time to the Canadian e-reader company Kobo, Inc. Borders had built far too many physical locations (many more than Barnes & Noble), which there was no need for, especially in an era heading toward digital. While the industry shifted, Borders didn't. The bookstore ultimately filed for bankruptcy in February 2011 and closed its 625 retail stores by September 2011.[8]

Not taking a risk is the riskiest thing you can do. Your company can't stand still as the world around it steadily churns forward with modernity. Just as people adapt in order to survive, so must your business.

ADAPTABILITY: SOCIAL TOOLS AND PRINCIPLES

Social media represents the most rapidly changing marketing landscape in human history, making adaptability key to survival. In fact, in a survey of Fortune 500 marketers, 94 percent cite the ability to adapt quickly to change as the most critical piece of social media success.[9] MySpace would have been a key network for your business to get involved with four year ago; today it is meaningless. Pinterest didn't exist 1½ years ago; now it's the third largest social network in the United States. And even "longtime" social networks such as Facebook and Twitter change rapidly, introducing new products and features nearly every month.

With social strategies and tools, you must be able to analyze and adapt to data and feedback. You must have a social media crisis response plan in order to react quickly to snafus such as the one that arose from Kenneth Cole's insensitive tweet last spring: "Millions are in uproar in #Cairo. Rumor is they heard our spring collection is now available online."

The company that does well in social media is able to build a nimble team of people who truly love social media, people who stay up late each night reading blogs and tweets and devouring information about new networks, products, and tools, so that you might consider them for your business.

Finally, consider developing your company blog on your own website. With social networks changing as much as they have over the past eight years, it becomes increasingly important to build a social following on your own website, which you'll control. You'll still have to adapt to changing networks, but you'll have the safety net of your own website and community to fall back on.

ACTION ITEMS

1. Brainstorm and write down five things you could be doing for your customers that you're not doing today.
2. Write down one risk you can take that might significantly benefit your company.
3. Hold a meeting with your team. Go around the room and have everyone offer one way you can improve the company. Write the suggestions down, pick one, and make it happen!

EMBRACE CHANGE
(OR IT WILL EMBRACE YOU)

The more success you have and the bigger your company grows, the harder it is to be nimble and flexible enough to effectively react to your changing environment. But as long as you're open to—rather than resistant to—change, your business will always be able to learn, adapt, and succeed. So don't merely get used to a constant state of flux; thrive in it.

CHAPTER 8

Passion

Love the Work You're With

The only way to do great work is to love what you do.

—Steve Jobs

Fifteen lousy bucks.

That's how much I earned my first night on the job selling Crunch 'n Munch in the fall of 2006. While in college at Boston University, I had taken a job as a vendor at Fenway Park and the Boston Garden (then known as the Fleet Center). I was a snack hawker who walked up and down the aisles selling product. What most people don't know is that vendors are paid only in commission and tips—the more they sell, the more they make. My first day, as the lowest man in the pecking order, seniority-wise, I had been assigned a product called "Crunch 'n Munch." I sold a grand total of 12 boxes and made the legal minimum, $15.

I decided later that night that while it was fun being at games, I wanted to at least make a decent living hawking Crunch 'n Munch. So my second day, I put some passion into my work— a little singing, a little dancing, a little screaming, and a lot of goofy Dave. I sold 36 boxes, three times as many as the first night. I stepped up my efforts for the rest of the week. The thing is, I'd be the first person to admit that I had no real talent as an entertainer. My only asset was passion, and perhaps fearlessness. I began to scream at the top of my lungs each night in an effort to pull attention away from the game people paid to see and toward the buttery toffee popcorn with peanuts I was selling (see Figure 8.1).

Passion paid off. Within weeks I had developed a persona as the "Crunch 'n Munch Guy," and regulars began to take notice. The in-stadium cameramen liked my shtick and began to feature my goofy dancing on the large-screen Jumbotron during time-outs. After the *Boston Herald* published its first article about me,[1] fans actually started asking me to autograph boxes of Crunch 'n Munch.

FIGURE 8.1 **Let's just say I had a passion for Crunch 'n Munch.**
Source: Dave Kerpen

Over the next three years, I was featured in the *Boston Herald*, *Boston Globe*, *Boston Magazine*, Fox Sports New England, ESPN, and dozens of other media outlets. I also sold *a lot* of Crunch 'n Munch. At my peak, I was selling between 250 and 300 boxes per game and making, with commission and tips, between $400 and $500 a night—an excellent living for a college kid. There I was, utterly talentless, but using my passion to sell. Management consultant Richard Whiteley even wrote in his 2001 book *Love the Work You're With*: "Like Dave Kerpen, we can break out of self-imposed or externally implied expectations, figure out ways to snap open our passion, and then put it into whatever it is we do."[2] Again, I assure you, I have no doubt that this was a case of passion trumping talent. But I never forgot how powerful that could be. Years later, as the CEO of a marketing firm, I don't need a horde of Likeable staff running around screaming and singing about social media in order to drum up business. But I do need people who care—people who put 110 percent into their work, people who see themselves not in a job but in a career, people who truly love the work they're with, people with passion. That's exactly why we made passion one of our core values at Likeable.

A PASSION FOR YOUR MISSION

Ben Cohen and Jerry Greenfield had always been passionate about creating peace in the world, and when they decided to open a business together, they turned their passion into a mission. They were steadfast in their belief that their business didn't have to take advantage of anyone to succeed and that they could make a reasonable profit while giving back to the community. That belief transferred to the creation of a great product that people would enjoy. Their business, Ben & Jerry's, is now a thriving, internationally popular ice cream company whose team still holds onto start-up–level passion decades later.

Sean Greenwood, the Ben & Jerry's PR manager, attributes the company's passion to employees' dedication to the Ben & Jerry's mission statement. The mission statement has three components:

social, product, and economic, and each one provides inspiration for the company as it continues to grow. From their website: "Underlying the mission of Ben & Jerry's is the determination to seek new and creative ways of addressing all three parts, while holding a deep respect for individuals inside and outside the company and for the communities of which they are a part."

Every Ben & Jerry's employee, from C-level management to ice-cream servers, is expected to help carry out the company's mission to the best of his or her ability. "Passion is important," Sean said to me. "Without it, work becomes mundane and boring. Just selling ice cream to sell ice cream would feel hollow. We have our causes and issues to support as a company and give individuals a way to support a cause. All of us have to earn a living, but if we can do it in a way that lets us help the community, it helps people feel better about what they're doing. The ability to employ passion in what you're doing is a great side effect of working at Ben & Jerry's."

But how does Ben & Jerry's, an international company with thousands of employees, keep those employees dedicated to its mission? By doing two things: innovating and forming connections.

If you're familiar with Ben & Jerry's, you may have noticed that the company is constantly creating new products. The nearly endless flavor combinations provide an outlet for Ben & Jerry's to innovate and try new things. But Ben & Jerry's doesn't limit innovation to its product line; the team is constantly coming up with new social initiatives as well. This is where forming connections comes in. The Social Mission department sends out surveys to Ben & Jerry's employees to get a feel for the issues that matter most to them. The department then uses the results of that survey along with other research to determine which charitable or social causes the company should support. Ben & Jerry's also grants employees five paid days off work to volunteer for the organization or cause of their choice. Because employees have a voice and an impact on the company's decisions, they feel a stronger connection to it.

Passion for the mission makes every employee's work that much easier. Employees can become passionate about things like packaging or serving ice cream if they're first passionate about the overall mission.

THE POWER OF PASSION

Passion is vital to your success. It invigorates, it provides purpose, and it focuses and shapes your work. It fulfills and provides value and worth to what you do. It makes a job not a job but a life's work.

While on a business trip to Italy, Howard Schultz stumbled across his passion in an espresso bar: "I was taken by the power that savoring a simple cup of coffee can have to connect people and create community among them, and from that moment on I was determined to bring world-class coffee and the romance of Italian espresso bars to the United States."[3] Schultz presented this idea to the heads of Starbucks, who ultimately turned him down. So he opened up his own coffee shop, eventually returning to buy out Starbucks and live out his dream.

Schultz's success can be attributed to his intense passion for coffee, a passion that has spread to each and every Starbucks barista and loyal customer. Before Schultz's Starbucks, coffee wasn't something American consumers were passionate about. But with his unwavering passion, Schultz was able to inspire thousands of employees and customers to study and fall in love with the bean, the drink, and the entire experience of drinking a cup of coffee.

DISCOVER YOUR PASSION

Schultz discovered his passion in an instant, the moment he walked into that Italian espresso bar. Others aren't as lucky and are still in search of their life's purpose.

But no matter where in life you are, it's never too late—or too early—to find passion in your career. It's not easy for many people, so if *you* are one of the many, consider putting this book down and taking some time to really reflect and work on discovering your passions. After all, life isn't just about building a likeable business, it's about building a valuable life for yourself and your family. I can't think of a lot of things more important than living a life filled with passion.

Passion isn't inherent in a job; it's found within the person. You have to reach inside yourself to discover it. Identify what motivates and engages you. It's your reason for living, the core of your soul. Knowing your passion will help drive your business and your success. It will give focus and purpose to what you do. No matter what your age and experience, if you haven't found your passion yet, I highly recommend the book *What Color Is Your Parachute?* to help find work you will love.

A PASSION FOR TEACHING

Steve Feldman is the founder and educational director of Private Prep, a tutoring service that offers unique lessons and standardized test prep for students in grades K–12. When Steve was growing up, his mom was a math teacher and popular math tutor. When Steve got to high school, he was a strong math student and began tutoring formally with his mom. During college, he would come home for the summer in time for finals at the high school and tutor students. When Steve graduated, he moved to New York City and got a job in finance, knowing that teaching wasn't a career that could easily support a family. He soon realized his heart wasn't in his job, and he began to miss teaching math and helping others. So he began tutoring after work, soon developing a reputation. When he had more clients than he could handle, Steve recruited friends to help. Realizing that his passion to teach could become a business, Steve left his job in the summer of 2006 and opened Private Prep in the fall. Three years later, passion-filled Steve had a business with over $1 million in annual sales.

You have to try things out, find what motivates you, what pushes you, what fuels your energy, what gets you excited—at work and in life. Find the happy meeting ground between loving something, being good at something, and having others be passionate about that thing too. And once you truly find your passion—ignite it.

Steve's advice for people who don't love what they're doing is simple: "Walk away," he says. "Follow your passion and what you *do* love. When you find what drives you, if you love what you do, you won't work a day in your life." Steve amended his statement: "That's not entirely true. It's demanding, but you never go to work not looking forward to it. You have a happier life when you enjoy what you do. Find what excites you and what makes you happy. When you find that, then you'll be more successful yourself. People feed off of that energy and passion, and it makes for a better life."

When Steve started hiring additional tutors, he asked his students what they liked about him as a tutor and what he should look for in applicants. The response: "I know that you care. If I come to you and haven't finished my homework, I'll feel bad." So when Steve hires tutors, the first thing he looks for is people who truly care. He noticed that great tutors leave an impression on students because the students recognize how passionately the tutors want to help. If the tutors are invested in the students, the students will be invested in themselves. Steve says that he and his tutors receive letters and e-mails from students all the time thanking them and letting them know that they got an A on a test or were accepted to a great university. Their passion also means that they never have to put effort into selling their services because it speaks for itself. "If passion is true and comes from an honest place, you don't need to sell anyone on it," Steve says. "People sense your passion and want to be a part of it." Steve explained that passion in general is contagious and rubs off on the tutors that he hires into the organization. And, of course, having passion for what you're doing helps make the experience more enjoyable. (See Figure 8.2.)

The most important thing is that your passion be real, because you can't fake it. People identify with people who are honest with themselves. At Private Prep, students can tell whether or not tutors are actually passionate about what they're

FIGURE 8.2   **Tutors at Private Prep have an undeniable passion for teaching.**
Source: Steve Feldman

doing. Steve says that when you're working with students, you have to be genuine; when you demonstrate passion and actually care about success, that shows through. If the students know that the tutors genuinely care about them, they will make a much bigger effort to succeed. The passion and emotion are contagious, and they motivate everyone—students and tutors alike—to make a stronger effort. The same idea holds true for any business: when employees can tell that their managers and leaders truly care about them and want to see them succeed, they will make a more conscious effort to contribute to the organization. Passion can make or break a small-business owner. If you have passion for your business and the problems you're solving for your customers, that will be contagious. If you don't, well, that will be contagious too.

PASSION FOR YOUR PRODUCT

In 1996, Peter van Stolk wanted to bring something new to the beverage industry. He felt it was time to introduce alternatives to the standard cola and lemon-lime-flavored carbonated drinks, flavors like Blue Bubblegum, FuFu Berry, and Bug Juice. Thus, a "rebel" was born in the form of Jones Soda.

The company developed a loyal following by resonating with like-minded, alternative-thinking, similarly passionate consumers on the fringe. The soda started popping up in surf and music stores, available only to people "in the know," people who connected with the brand and loved its uniqueness as much as the company did.

Inevitably, word spread, and Jones Soda rapidly outgrew its "small business" label, bringing in over $12 million in 2011. So how did a young, rebellious company maintain its inspiration, passion, and edge while going mainstream? It gave its brand over to its brand lovers. Just take a look at one of the bottles: besides the logo and basic layout, each and every Jones Soda label features a photo from a member of its community—there are photos of skaters, of friends, of art, of life (see Figure 8.3). "If I put your photo on something you love," Peter says, "whatever that may be—on a bottle of Jones Soda—you'll actually care, because it's your photo, not mine."[4] The entire collection of over 40,000 photos forms a collage of what the company represents to the real people who have a real love for the product.

"A soda company just means that you're a carbonated soft drink or a beverage with sugar and bubbles," Peter says. "I think Jones means more than that."

Passion creates brand communities, loyal groups of customers evangelizing for the company. Find the passionate ones. Find the ones who could love your product, and give them a reason to love it. Light their fire. Find the ones who could believe in your product, and give them a reason to believe.

As a business leader, you have to believe in your product and company, because if you don't, how can your customers or employees? More important, you have to believe in, and live out, your mission. And your mission can't be to make a lot of money.

FIGURE 8.3 Jones Soda showcases its passionate fan base.
Source: Cliff Sebastian

If you're driven not by your passion but by money, you can't have a successful business.

Facebook earned $3.7 billion in 2011 revenue, and in its May 2012 IPO, CEO Mark Zuckerberg instantly became worth more than $17 billion. It's stock has since plummeted, and many have questioned how valuable Facebook really is. But the hoodie-and-jeans–wearing 27-year-old couldn't care less about the money. What Zuckerberg cares about is Facebook's mission.

In his letter to investors included in the IPO filing, Zuck writes, "Facebook was not originally created to be a company. It was built to accomplish a social mission—to make the world more open and connected."[5] When Zuck launched Facebook from his Harvard dorm room in 2004, he didn't envision building a company. In fact, he once told a friend via instant messaging, "Well, I don't know business stuff. I'm content to make something cool."[6]

That contentment remained during his move to Silicon Valley, with Zuck still not focusing on the fact that he would be starting a company. All that mattered to him was continuing to work on a project he believed in. As he once observed, "If you start to build something . . . it's hard, and you encounter a lot of challenges. If you don't completely love and believe in what you're doing, it actually ends up being the rational thing for you to stop doing it or succumb to some of the challenges."[7] Facebook won't employ people who don't love or believe in what they do. The company looks for people who are passionate about something, anything, enough to have shown the initiative to take that passion and run with it, creating something on their own, driven only by love of their work.

In his letter to investors mentioned above, Zuck explains very clearly Facebook's mission-driven purpose: "We don't build services to make money. We make money to build better services." Facebook's CEO isn't passionate about earning profits or taking over the world; he's passionate about "building something cool," something that can connect the world. And his intense focus on that mission is what has driven Facebook to its great success. Don't let your company's vision become myopic, don't fall out of love with what you do, and don't lose the spark that once lit your business's fire. As Steve Jobs once advised, "Stay hungry. Stay foolish."[8] Stay start-up–like. Stay inspired. Stay passionate.

PASSION IN POLITICS

The 2008 election was a whirlwind of change and media blitz. The economy was low, emotions were high, and the whole country was in a tizzy. When the primaries ended and the dust cleared, an Illinois senator named Barack Obama emerged as the front-runner for the Democratic Party. Obama traveled the United States speaking of hope, promise, and change. His passion, unmatched by candidates from the Republican Party, filled the hearts of millions of Americans and inspired them to donate money and volunteer for his campaign. Obama's passion for change in America spread over social media as he reached out to young voters, igniting their passion for politics and voting. A candidacy that once seemed like a shot in the dark was becoming a real possibility.

On election night, Americans watched as state after state turned either blue or red on the United States map. When the results were in, Barack Obama was the forty-fourth president of the United States and the first African American president in American history. But it wasn't his policies or ideas that drove the election; it was his passion. Obama's contagious passion for his campaign and the future of America spread to voters across the nation via his impassioned speeches and inspired vision. Even Republicans would agree that Obama set the standard for passion in politics.

Passion lives best visually, when your audience can literally see the passion emanating from your face and your body language. Scaling passion means being present, even if it's not in person. For instance, CEOs may address large groups of staff via video or team huddles to start off each week. If Obama's 2008 presidential campaign tells us anything, it's that passion is scalable and can spread to incredible numbers of people. If a senator can convert his passion into a successful election, a business leader can certainly use it to build a thriving business.

PASS YOUR PASSION ON

David Holmes is a flight attendant for Southwest Airlines, an airline known for its fun, energetic staff, sense of humor, and dedication to making flying a unique and enjoyable experience. David is the embodiment of what Southwest stands for as a company. When passengers board the plane, he gives them a big smile and welcomes them aboard. Once all the passengers have boarded and gotten situated, the real fun begins. "I've had five flights today, and I just cannot do the regular boring announcement again," David tells the passengers. "Otherwise I'm gonna

put myself to sleep." He then asks the passengers to start laying down a beat by stomping and clapping. Once the audience
has established a rhythm, David raps the before-flight instructions, from beverage options to take-off procedures. There are
big smiles all around as David finishes his "announcement," and
the passengers give him a round of applause.

David doesn't always rap the in-flight instructions, as he
explained in an interview with the *Wall Street Journal*. "I don't
do it on a 6 a.m. flight," he said. "Nobody wants to hear it at
that time. I'm risking getting a beating doing that at six in the
morning."[9] Of course, David doesn't have to rap the instructions
at all; it's not in the employee handbook. He does it because he
enjoys it, and it puts a smile on passengers' faces. David's passion for his job is immediately evident to passengers, and the
unexpected surprise adds a lot of value to the experience of flying on Southwest.

David's not the only passionate employee at Southwest
Airlines. Southwest has the highest employee retention rate of
any airline, with a turnover rate of only 4 percent. Additionally,
Southwest has never had a mass layoff. Finally, despite the fact
that Southwest consistently charges very low fares, it's the only
consistently profitable airline since 1973. Southwest ranks top in
customer service, and it shows in consumer loyalty. People who
fly on Southwest are consistently treated with excellent customer
service from passionate employees, and they keep coming back
for more.

WITH PASSION, EVERYONE AT
YOUR COMPANY IS A MARKETER

Passion is contagious, compelling everyone around you who
experiences it to jump on board. Everyone at your company is a
marketer: if an engineer or any nonsalesperson talks about how
much he or she loves your product or company, and someone
overhears it, that could lead to business. Find the right people.
At Likeable, I would rather have an employee who is passionate
about what we do than someone who is smarter but less passion-

ate. Truly great employees and business leaders are motivated by creating valuable, great work rather than by making money.

Create an environment where people are willing, able, and compelled to carry out your mission. Passionate employees will be self-motivated and geared up each day to do great work. And the second you know someone on your staff isn't passionate about the work he or she is doing, you have to extinguish that flickering flame; a lack of passion is a virus that infiltrates.

IF IT'S JUST A JOB, FIND ANOTHER ONE

At a recent Likeable management retreat, our president, Carrie, asked each manager to define his or her dream role at the company. We went around the boardroom, and each person shared. Most people indicated they were currently in their dream roles (lucky for us!), but a couple of people described dream jobs a bit different from their current roles at the organization. One person described her current role with a clear lack of enthusiasm.

"This is your chance to describe your dream job," said Carrie. "Why no excitement?"

"Well, it's just a job," she responded.

The minute we heard that, Carrie and I knew that she didn't have the passion for Likeable that we need in every employee. And that's really okay. Many managers and business owners struggle with this problem. Rather than letting passionless employees go, they futilely try to ignite passion. Instead, we can help such employees find their passion elsewhere. I gave the passionless employee a copy of *What Color Is Your Parachute*, and we worked out a plan to help find her another job, one that isn't "just a job."

I truly believe that the words "It's just a job" need not ever be uttered, because for every organization on the planet, and maybe even for every job, there are people who are deeply passionate. From ballpark vendor to flight attendant to senior manager, from Fortune 500 company to start-up, from global nonprofit to tiny government agency, there is someplace for everybody. Our job as leaders is to find the people with passion for our organizations and jobs—and when we miss the mark, we should help those people find their passions elsewhere. In the end, this works out best not only for our organizations, but also for the employees in question.

INJECTING PASSION INTO YOUR WORK

In 1992, Richard Whiteley, cofounder and vice chairman of the Forum Corporation, noticed his passion was dwindling. Once excited to manage others, he now found it a burden. So he decided to assess the various aspects of his job, listing the pluses—marketing, mentoring, writing, and public speaking—and minuses—budgeting, managing, and attending meetings. After he finished, he made a concerted effort to do more of the pluses and less of the minuses to bring his work into balance and reinvigorate his passion. Ultimately, he gave up his position as division president and cut his work time at the company by half, resulting in a 50 percent pay decrease. But this trade-off allowed Richard more time to do the things he truly loved to do, regaining his passion.[10]

Sometimes the passion just isn't there, or it starts to fade after time. If you're a business leader, maybe you've lost your initial spark, or maybe your employees are weighed down by routine, and their hearts aren't in it anymore.

Everyone is motivated by something. It may not be the existing parameters of a job, the money, the manager, or the responsibilities, but figuring out what that thing is will open up passion. Do more of what you love and less of what stands in the way of it. Get out of the way of your passion.

WHEN THE PASSION ISN'T THERE

Steve Jobs had a passion not just for technology but for making the world a better place through technology. In 1983, he persuaded John Sculley to leave Pepsi to serve as Apple's CEO by asking him, "Do you want to sell sugar water for the rest of your life, or do you want to come with me and change the world?"[11] Ironically, it was contention with Sculley that led to Jobs being fired by Apple's board of directors, who, between 1985 and 1997, appointed a series of CEOs who lacked Jobs's vision and love for Apple. When a CEO loves his company and what it does, that is obvious, motivating the entire company and making customers believe in the company. When Jobs rejoined Apple, he brought the company back from the brink of bankruptcy, revitalized the brand, and turned Apple into the highly prolific brand it is today. It's now a brand that consumers rally around and become passionate about. (In fact, studies have proven that consumers actually love their iPhones, releasing the same hormones as when they're in love.) Such success can be achieved only when a leader is passionately championing the business. If he or she doesn't love it, why should anyone else?

Carol Bartz, former CEO at Yahoo, was spectacularly ousted from the company in the fall of 2011. Her infamously enraged reaction to the firing phone call and her recounting of it to the press were more passionate than her leadership of the company—and that was exactly the problem. Bartz didn't work out because she had no passion for what Yahoo did, and she didn't attempt to spark a passion or reenvision the company to be in line with what she did love. She worked at a company she wasn't truly interested or invested in. Her passion didn't align, and she ultimately floundered as a result.

People without passion are just doing their jobs, not their life's work. And that's why those who don't have passion often flounder—because they allow failure to even be an option. And Marissa Mayer won't. In July 2012, Marissa was named as Yahoo's new CEO. In stark contrast to Carol Bartz, Marissa is as passionate as it gets. She once said that passion is a gender-neutralizing force. And proudly toting her "geek" status, for her, the CEO title only means, "for an area that you're passionate about, all the details matter." And every detail does: the Google employee number 20 was so committed to the company, she's not unfamiliar with 130-hour workweeks. If anyone has the passion to succeed at the helm of a flailing tech company, it's Marissa Mayer.

A leader not in love with his or her business has no place there. People don't follow leaders who have no passion, and no amount of money or rewards can truly motivate a person without passion. If you don't love what you do, you won't do it well.

PASSION: SOCIAL TOOLS AND PRINCIPLES

Passion is often best conveyed face-to-face. Your challenge online is to capture your passion and your team's passion and then to authentically share it online across social networks. Who is best suited at your company to represent you in social media? It may or may not be someone who works in marketing, but it should almost definitely be someone who is staunchly passionate about your organization and mission.

Our company's main representative on Twitter is Michele Weisman. Though Michele is not a founder and currently has no equity in the company, she's often quoted as saying she "bleeds orange," our company color. Michele is incredibly passionate about Likeable and our mission, and that passion shows in every tweet, Instagram pic, and Pinterest pin she sends out.

Just as you can't fake passion in the offline world, you can't fake passion on social networks. Your followers will be able to deduce how much you care based on how quickly you respond to social media interactions and how comprehensive your social media presence is.

One awesome aspect of social media is that you can convey your passion to many people with one click of your mouse. In the past, passion was most often shared offline, in the boardroom or on the golf course. Today, once you've built up a sizable audience across social networks, you can share your passion with hundreds, thousands, or even millions of people at once, who can in turn share their passion for you with their own audiences.

ACTION ITEMS

1. Write down five things you're passionate about in life and business. If you died doing what you love, what would that be?
2. Determine three ways you can inject more passion into your work today; then do it!
3. Determine three ways you can inspire more passion in your company.

4. Connect with your customers' passion. Understand what they love and care about and how you can play a part in that.

LOVE THE WORK YOU'RE WITH—OR QUIT

Figure out what you're truly passionate about, and harness that passion to drive your success. If you don't love what you do, you won't do it well. As Steve Jobs once advised, "If you don't love it, you're going to give up." Ultimately, passion fuels the perseverance needed to succeed. Find your inner passion in what you do now—or quit and find your passion somewhere else. Then make sure the other members of your team have passion for their organization and jobs. Remember, both passion *and lack of passion* are contagious.

CHAPTER 9

Surprise and Delight
Every Mistake Is an Opportunity

A true leader always keeps an element of surprise up his sleeve, which others cannot grasp but which keeps his public excited and breathless.

—Charles de Gaulle

Victor Gonzalez was among the millions of Twitter users who have tweeted at celebrities, attempting to get a response, usually to no avail. In Victor's case, the celebrity was New England Patriots wide receiver Chad Ochocinco. Eventually fed up with being ignored, Victor sent Ochocinco the following tweet: "Been tweeting at you for two years and have not ever gotten a response."

This caught the football star's attention. Ochocinco owned up to his unresponsiveness, promptly tweeting back: "Damn 2 years? My bad. Want to come to the game Saturday?"

Well, that was a no-brainer for Victor; of course he did! Unfortunately, he was a college student in Florida and was unable to make it up to Massachusetts. "I would love to but I live in FLA," he jokingly tweeted back. "Can you fly me out? Lol."

Ochocinco *actually agreed to this* and told Victor that someone would be in touch shortly to make the arrangements.

Nowhere in Chad Ochocinco's contract does it say that he has to fly a fan to a game for free. And Victor Gonzalez probably would have been content with a brief Twitter exchange with his favorite player. But Ochocinco went the extra mile to show one fan how much he appreciated him and, with the power of social media, was able to show all his fans how he feels about them. It was an easy thing to do, but something no one else was doing, and the gesture set Ochocinco apart, giving him a reputation as a responsive, appreciative, stand-up athlete. Additionally, Ochocinco's story was featured by more than 60 media outlets, generating millions of dollars in earned media—and surely helping his chances at future endorsement deals.

JUST DELIGHTFUL

Delight doesn't have to involve a mind-blowing surprise. In fact, it shouldn't, generally. Customers shouldn't be surprised by a delightful moment with your company; they should come to expect it from you. Being delightful is about creating a remarkable customer experience. Delight is when an Apple customer buys an iPad and has a beautiful, pleasant experience opening the box. Delight is when shoppers walk down the aisles of Fairway Supermarkets in New York or Stu Leonard's in Connecticut. Delight is when a customer is able to enjoy personal service when purchasing a product.

Imagine you're in a frenzy on a Saturday morning with a long list of errands, including taking your kids to get haircuts and depositing a check. You rush to your bank, kids in tow, before it closes at noon. After battling heavy traffic, you pull up to the teller's window at exactly 12:01. Instead of flipping over the "Sorry, we're closed" sign, the teller smiles and says brightly, "Good morning! What can I do for you today?" You tell her, and she promptly hands you a deposit slip and a pen, which she says you can keep. After you hand the slip back, she says, "It'll be just a moment," and it actually is. She hands you a receipt and lollipops for your kids before sending you on your way. While that may sound like a fairy tale, the tellers at BBVA Compass bank do that sort of thing every day. They're prompt and positive and genuinely care about creating a satisfactory and delightful customer experience. If you need to go inside a branch to chat about a loan or open a savings account, you're welcome to help yourself to a bag of free popcorn from the popcorn machine. A $3.4 billion financial holding company with a top-ranked reputation, the Birmingham-based bank has over 8,800 employees and is one of the 25 largest banks in the United States, but that doesn't stop BBVA from having a small-town feel where customers are cared for and delivered an enjoyable experience every time.

Unfortunately, the opposite kind of experience probably comes to mind far more easily, not just at banks but at many establishments. Remember the time you waited in a long line for your morning caffeine boost, only to get the wrong order; and then when you sheepishly pointed out the missing soy and your lactose intolerance to your barista, she begrudgingly remade your drink and threw it at you, ignoring your expression of gratitude? Or the time when your request for "No pickles on that Number 5, please" was translated into "Give me all the pickles you have on that Number 5, please"?

And what about going to the Department of Motor Vehicles? Few would argue that this is one of the least delightful experiences on the planet. You wake up absurdly early, stand in line for an hour, take a number, sit and wait, watching two hours' worth of infomercials, just so you can get your picture retaken and vision tested in the span of eight minutes. It's a chore that has to be powered through, one of life's necessary evils. Companies need to be thinking of ways to turn experiences that customers dread into bearable and then enjoyable ones. And what's worse is when your customer experience isn't a "necessary evil" but just "evil"; your customers will flee. Statistics show that 40 percent of customers will leave a business in response to a poor experience. Creating delightful interactions between your company and your customers is what will make them enjoy doing business with you and keep them coming back for more.

THE ELEMENT OF SURPRISE

What's the difference between a delight and a delightful surprise? A delight is a meal at your favorite gourmet restaurant. A delightful surprise is when a delicious dessert is served, compliments of the chef.

Surprise, of course, doesn't have to involve giving away free food. Adding the element of surprise to your business just requires overdelivering and exceeding your customers' expectations.

Zappos is an online clothing and shoe retailer now operating under the Amazon umbrella. The company's core value is to "Deliver WOW through customer service." Driven by this mission, Zappos uses its customer service to overdeliver and surprise buyers. Zappos offers free four-day shipping. Always getting products to customers on time would constitute consistent, delightful customer service. But Zappos does even better, getting shoppers their purchases sooner, sometimes even by the very next day.

The company also offers free returns, which is certainly delightful but doesn't quite live up to the promise of being "exceptional." Something truly amazing? Zappos once sent a free pair of shoes to a best man who arrived at a wedding shoeless. In another case, Zappos sent a flower bouquet to a woman who returned a pair of boots for her husband because he had died in a car accident. Once, a customer service rep went to a rival shoe store to find a specific pair of shoes for a customer staying at a nearby hotel after Zappos ran out of stock. Zappos has hundreds of glowing reviews and customer testimonials on its site and has many loyal customers, all because of its commitment to making sure every single person who orders from the company has a spectacular experience. Zappos has grown to be the largest online shoe store, with 75 percent of its daily sales coming from repeat buyers.[1] The primary source of the company's success has been word-of-mouth recommendations due to its delightful customer service reputation.

SURPRISE AND DELIGHT THROUGH
SOCIAL MEDIA

Social media allows for surprise and delight at scale, reaching far beyond the one customer with whom you have that special interaction. When you deliver exceptional customer service or surprise a customer with a free product, that customer is going to be compelled to share that delight with his or her friends and followers. When the whole world is watching, it's not just a single customer you're surprising and delighting.

In November 2010, Dutch airline KLM launched a campaign to "spread happiness," surprising travelers who checked in on foursquare with a personal gift that could make their trip more enjoyable and less stressful. The second a passenger checked in at one of KLM's locations at its main hub, Amsterdam Schiphol Airport, the "Surprise Team" started researching the person using information he or she publicly published online. From this, the team was able to determine the perfect customized gift. One customer was going to miss his favorite soccer team's biggest game of the year while on a trip to New York. So the KLM team surprised him with a Lonely Planet guide to New York, highlighting the best bars to watch the game. The team learned that another passenger was celebrating his birthday and surprised him with a card and a glass of champagne. KLM was committed to making customers' days and was interested in seeing how the small bits of happiness the airline created for individuals could spread via social media and word-of-mouth. And spread they did: KLM earned over 1 million impressions, was cited as a best-practice example by the BBC and multiple other media sources, and is now a top-rated airline for customer service, all from using a delightful surprise to show how it cared about and valued its customers.[2]

An important aspect of the element of surprise is the psychology of variable rewards. Behavioral psychologist B. F. Skinner discovered that behavior reinforced intermittently is the most difficult to extinguish. It's what makes playing a slot machine so addictive: you know the win will come, but you're just not sure when, and so you keep pulling the handle, trying to increase your chances. What does that mean for you as a business leader? You've got to find a way to get people to start "playing the slot machines." If you surprise and delight some employees and some customers, people will be drawn to you, hoping to get their chance, constantly wondering, "When will be my turn? How can I be next?"

FREE IS LIKE MAGIC

The burrito company Boloco has frequent internal discussions about how each and every day, every single person at the company is empowered to amaze people. It starts with the little things, the things that should happen every day, everywhere: greeting guests with a genuine smile, sincerely wanting to help those unfamiliar with the menu. The next step is making up for a nondelightful customer experience: Boloco not only corrects its human mistakes; it goes above and beyond, offering a free menu item or two. Customers have definitely been surprised at the extreme to which the company takes customer service. When feedback about a poor experience gets to the ears of CEO John Pepper, it's basically game over: "They're about to get more freebies than they know what to do with." People can, and do, surely take advantage of this, but Pepper doesn't mind: "We're not going to ask for proof, and we're not going to stop being overly giving just because we know people are taking advantage of us."

Just making up for mistakes isn't enough for Boloco. It takes surprise and delight one step further with celebratory events. On customers' birthdays, they each receive a free menu item. Delightful, right? Well, that's nothing compared to what Boloco recently did on the company's own birthday. To celebrate 15 years in business, Boloco organized a series of 15 Free Burrito Days at its various locations (see Figure 9.1). That's 15 full days of customers lining up for an entire day outside a specified Boloco location for a free burrito (or two). Free Burrito Days aren't anything new; the company has been doing them regularly since 2009 to show appreciation for its community and customers.

FIGURE 9.1 **Customers swarm Boloco stores on Free Burrito Day.**
Source: John Pepper

Pepper does Free Burrito Days based on a gut instinct that they are the right thing to do for Boloco. As opposed to discounts that can devalue a brand, Pepper believes "free" to be a magic word. Unlike "50 percent off," "free" is truly delightful to people, and customers will wait in exorbitantly long lines for a free item. Of course, Free Burrito Days just so happen to have a positive effect on Boloco's bottom line. After each Free Burrito Day, the company's volume of business experiences a lift, and Boloco has grown in popularity year after year. According to a 2011 study on the promotion, Dartmouth College Tuck School of Business determined that a Free Burrito Day pays for itself in about 15 days. The study also found that on days following a Free Burrito Day in 2010, Boloco saw a 20 percent increase in comparable sales; and following that, Boloco saw a 10 percent increase in permanent sales. In 2012, Boloco handed out exactly 37,600 freebies (a total of $110,000 in burritos) and, as an extra good deed for the community, raised $20,717 for Life Is Good Playmakers, a nonprofit foundation of Boston-based apparel company Life Is Good.

Forget merely surprising customers. Boloco gave them an absolute *shock* with this year's annual April Fool's joke. On April 1, 2012, Boloco sent out an e-mail to its customers containing a message from Pepper. The e-mail explained that the first 13 of the 15 Free Burrito Days were costing four times as much as the company had planned for. "And as icing on the cake," he added, "the utility bills in late March for never-before-needed air conditioning were extraordinary." So Pepper said that Boloco would be canceling the final two Free Burrito Days effective immediately, the money currently raised for the Life Is Good Playmakers would go toward utility bills, and Boloco would be taking away any freebies it had put on customers' cards, as well as adding a $0.25 surcharge to all future orders to make up for the company's losses. Oh, and P.S., April Fool's! Pepper then explained it was all a joke, life is good, and Boloco would be putting an additional mini burrito on every customer's card as an extra surprise.

Granted, some missed the fact that the e-mail was a joke, including Pepper's own mother. The fact that customers could believe Boloco would do such a terrible thing was unbelievable to Pepper. "It shows how little people think of businesses these days," he said. The company ended up giving away an extra $41,000 in burritos just for the sake of a little April Fool's fun for its valued customers. But as Pepper says, "The reason we do it is because we think Boloco is the place you can visit often enough that, over time, we can make up for the things we give away and have a good business because of it." It's a trade-off: giving away thousands of burritos in return for thousands of ecstatic, loyal customers.

EVERY CUSTOMER ISN'T CREATED EQUAL

There is no Declaration of Consumers' Independence that says, "Every customer is created equal." As repeat buyers and brand evangelists, loyal customers are more valuable to a company than other customers. And in today's social media age, an influential customer with a large, captive audience is particularly important. Since it's physically impossible to surprise every one of your customers—not to mention the fact that if you surprised everyone, it would no longer be a surprise but an expectation—you must select the people who will have the most influence on spreading the word and the greatest impact on increasing business. How do you determine who these people are? One method is to use Klout. The social media analytics service measures social media users' influence based on their ability to drive action from their audience. So if you have the choice between surprising and delighting a customer with a low Klout score and one with a high score, choose the greater influencer in order to reach the greatest number of people and get the biggest bang for your buck.

Or how about the person having a terrible, horrible, no-good day? When you surprise and delight that poor soul, he or she is going to be so overjoyed as to have no choice but to tell every Twitter follower, friend, coworker, and subway companion about the experience. The point is to strategically pick your people and your timing to create small moments of surprise and delight that will then spread and have the greatest impact on your business.

MY OPRAH MOMENTS; MAYBE IT'S NOT SUCH A WASTE OF MONEY

I've always been a big fan of surprise and delight—for both customers and staff. I enjoy randomly calling out employees who are doing a great job at team meetings with kudos and handing them a small gift card, or calling up an important customer and offering the customer a suite at a Mets game. It makes me feel good, and I can't help but think it has a positive effect on staff and clients.

It was a summer night in 2010 when my head began to spin with surprise-and-delight possibilities. I was at home with my wife, Carrie; the kids were asleep; and I was begrudgingly about to watch a DVR'd episode of *The Oprah Winfrey Show*.

"You're going to love this, Dave," Carrie said. "It's Oprah's 'favorite things' episode."

I had no idea what she was talking about, but I was intrigued enough to keep watching as Oprah surprised her studio guests with gift after gift, including jewelry, household appliances, books, and then a trip to Australia! The shock value alone made for incredible entertainment—and I just kept thinking about how much value she was adding to her guests' lives in just one hour.

I devised a plan to create "Dave's Favorite Things" to surprise and reward our super-hardworking, productive employees at our company holiday party. I put together a list of things I loved that our staff (20 people at the time) would likely enjoy as well—a Dunkin' Donuts gift card, Facebook swag, TOMS shoes, a Donors Choose gift card, and, finally, the kicker: a seven-day Norwegian cruise to the Bahamas. I was so excited. Of course, there was one catch—selling the idea to my wife and business partner. We wanted to keep it a surprise, and so we couldn't bring it to our finance staff. While it looked like we had the money in the bank to pay for it, obviously it would be a big expense. Would it really be worth it, or would it be a total waste of money?

The holiday party was in December. I'd prepared a PowerPoint deck that I'd told the team I was going to present at the party. The cover slide read "20 Things You Need to Know as the Company Prepares for 2011." I gathered everyone together and began the fake presentation. The second slide featured a screenshot of my head over Oprah with the caption "Dave's Favorite Things." I even cued up the song Oprah had used when she did her big reveal, "I've Got a Feeling" by the Black Eyed Peas.

The next 10 minutes were nothing short of mayhem. People couldn't believe that I'd kept it a surprise; and gift after gift, they freaked out with excitement, no matter the value of the prize. When we got to the cruise, people were moved to tears.

I had succeeded in having my Oprah moment—but was it worth it? What was the return on investment on that massive surprise-and-delight moment? Well, of course, it's hard to know how valuable that $30,000 investment was versus spending the same amount elsewhere. And though we gave away Amazon Kindle Fires and a trip to Miami to 35 people in 2011, it will be next to impossible to continue doing "Dave's Favorite Things" year after year as the company grows. But I can assure you, our team had an amazing time bonding together on that cruise, and our staff turnover is much lower than that of competitive agencies of the same size. We could have spent the same amount of money on increasing everyone's cash bonus, and that would have made our employees happy for sure. But delighted and fiercely loyal? No, it took an Oprah moment to do that.

Determine ways to surprise and delight your own employees. Even better, figure out how to create operationalized surprise and delight in scalable, cheaper ways. (You don't have to fly your staff to Miami to reward and invigorate them.) Your staff will start gushing about how great it is to work for your company. Word will spread, and you'll soon have great talent knocking on (and knocking down) your door.

WORD-OF-MOUTH-WORTHY

To get customers talking about your company, you need to give them something to talk about. A great topic is truly buzzworthy; it's organic, it's exceptional, and it makes people unable to *not* say something. There is nothing more word of mouth–worthy than surprising and delighting consumers. A delighted customer wants to share that joy with others and pass the happiness on, and a surprised customer can't help but express his or her shock over an unexpected event. When you can delight a customer every time or surprise key customers at some times, that's a word-of-mouth marketing gem. If you can consistently surprise and delight, that *is* your marketing. Word-of-mouth marketing happens on its own; you don't need to do an ad campaign. The word will spread, and you will be known as a likeable company.

Trader Joe's is a company that has grown in popularity almost solely due to word of mouth. The grocery store does very little marketing but has built a loyal fan base of customers eager to evangelize the brand. (Check out "I Made a Commercial for Trader Joe's" on YouTube, and you'll see what I mean.) Why? Because it is an exceptional company that consistently delights its shoppers. In 1977, founder Joseph Coulombe set out to create a place where people would enjoy shopping. Inspired by a trip to the Caribbean, he sought to make the grocery shopping experience feel like going on a vacation. Trader Joe's employees don Hawaiian shirts, hand out snacks and beverages from "tasting huts," and use nautical terminology: store managers are called "captains" and assistant managers "first mates." The stores feature quirky, hand-painted signage on the rustic, cedar-planked walls and sport an island-themed decor with a location-specific spin. (As you can see in Figure 9.2, the store on Boylston Street in Boston has an homage to Fenway Park at its entrance.) The company offers unique, buzzworthy products and pleasant policies: Do you want to mix and match your brews? Go right ahead. And returns? Sure thing, even if the products have been opened and you just didn't like how they tasted. The happy, helpful "crew members" are eager to assist at all times, sprinting down aisles to fetch products and grabbing bags of food you'd like to try.

Going grocery shopping is something consumers have to do; going to Trader Joe's is something consumers *get* to do. By turning a normally dreaded chore into an activity consumers look forward to being delighted by, Trader Joe's has created a loyal fan base of shoppers who can't keep their mouths shut about their favorite place to spend a Sunday afternoon.

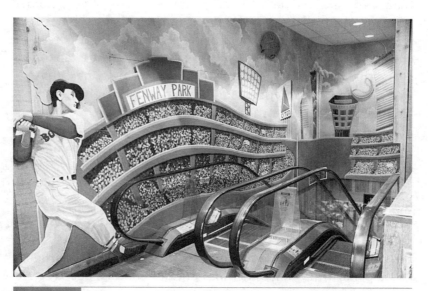

FIGURE 9.2 **The Trader Joe's on Boylston Street delightfully shows Boston pride.**
Source: DJ Switz

EVERY MISTAKE IS AN OPPORTUNITY
TO SURPRISE AND DELIGHT

"Why couldn't they get a simple cookie platter right?" I thought angrily as I prepared to dial the Star Service team at the Loews Royal Pacific Resort in Orlando, Florida.

I had planned a birthday celebration to remember for my daughter, Charlotte, at Universal Studios. Charlotte's a huge Harry Potter fan, so we had arranged for a VIP tour of Harry Potter World inside Universal, amongst lots of other surprises, such as a cookie platter and "Happy Birthday" sign at our hotel room at 4 p.m. On the way back to the hotel, I told Charlotte, "I think there might be something waiting for you in your room," and she got very excited.

So when we got back to the hotel room to find nothing, we were both disappointed. I called up "Star Service" thinking I was getting anything but that.

Cristina Bolanos, the assistant manager for Star Service, picked up, and I told her why I was upset.

"I'm sorry," she said. "We are working on the cookie platter and will send it right up."

"Well, thanks," I replied. "But the whole point was to surprise her for her birthday."

Cristina followed, totally validating how I was feeling: "I know, we really messed up. I love planning surprises for people and I know how upsetting it is when the surprise doesn't go as planned. Let me work on this. What is your daughter into?"

I told her Charlotte adored all things Harry Potter, and I thanked her. The cookies came up, and we enjoyed them, even though it was no longer a surprise.

A couple hours later, we got a note offering us complimentary breakfast the next morning. I thought this was a nice surprise for me, but obviously my nine-year-old couldn't really appreciate it.

The next morning, at breakfast, the hostess brought over to Charlotte a giant package of Harry Potter balloons tied to a jar of Gummi bears, along with a gift-wrapped box and card (see Figure 9.3).

FIGURE 9.3 **Surprising and delighting this nine-year-old yielded over 9,000 impressions online for the hotel.**
Source: Dave Kerpen

Charlotte freaked out in unexpected excitement and opened the box. Inside was an authentic Hermione Granger magic wand (a $50 item from Universal's Harry Potter World!). The card read, "Happy birthday, Charlotte! From Cristina and all of your friends at Loews."

I can't tell you how happy this made my daughter, and therefore me. Cristina had recognized an error the hotel had made, and then had gone ridiculously out of her way to make it right. I can't imagine that they had magic wands in inventory, which means someone had to go purchase it, wrap it, and set everything up.

In the process, I went from telling a story about how a Loews hotel couldn't get a cookie platter right to raving about Cristina and her truly "Star Service" to anyone who would listen. And writing about it here. And insisting upon staying at Loews hotels in the future whenever possible.

Everyone and every organization makes mistakes. But if you can follow up those mistakes with a little (or a lot) of surprise and delight, you can not only erase the mistakes—you can create fans for life. How much is that worth to you?

SURPRISE AND DELIGHT: SOCIAL TOOLS AND PRINCIPLES

The social media age has ushered in a new era of surprise and delight. It has always been a good idea to surprise and delight customers. But now that it is so easy for people to share their happiness with so many people across social networks, the surprise and delight of one customer can become the surprise and delight of the world. Use social tools to scale surprise and delight.

You probably can't surprise and delight all your online customers, so the notion of online influence becomes important. Klout, Kred, mPact, and other influence metrics tell you how influential various people are across the social web. Klout is the leading such service and assigns millions of people a score between 1 and 100 based on how likely their actions are to influence others online to take action (share, comment, retweet, like, etc.). According to Klout, the three most influential people online are Justin Bieber, Lady Gaga, and Barack Obama.

If a celebrity like George Clooney walked through the doors of your business or office, you'd probably give him special treatment, especially because you'd know he could have a huge influence on others for your business. Similarly, if someone with a huge Klout score interacts with you on a social network, that person could have a disproportionately large impact on your business, and therefore that person is worth surprising and delighting more than the average customer.

If you're able to figure out how to do little things for your online communities, delighting them and providing unexpected value, you will stand out, be memorable, and win social media users' business. It was important to be remarkable before the social media age, but today, when word can spread at the speed of light, it's absolutely essential.

ACTION ITEMS

1. Think of three delightful customer service experiences you've had recently. What do they all have in common? Create a plan to implement those elements into your business.
2. Write down five ways you can surprise your customers by going above and beyond their expectations.
3. Brainstorm ways you can surprise and delight your employees this year. Write down a plan to make one of them happen.
4. Write down one way you can be remarkable in an interaction with a customer today and one way you can be remarkable in an interaction with a colleague today. Then go be remarkable!

BE DELIGHTFUL AND SURPRISING

Surprising and delighting your customers and employees is one of the best ways to gain loyalty and word-of-mouth recognition. But don't do it for the repeat business (though that will result), and don't do it for the buzz (though that will come). Instead, do it for the same reason you throw a surprise party for a friend or send flowers to your mother: to show you truly care about and appreciate them. KLM's hypothesis was correct; happiness spreads. Happy customers and staff make for a happy business.

CHAPTER 10

Simplicity

Less isn't more; just enough is more.

—Milton Glaser

Joel Gascoigne was a big fan of Twitter, but he had one problem: he found it difficult to consistently tweet and share all the great articles he found. He tested various scheduling tools, but they all just made things more complicated: you had to pick the date and time, fiddle with a schedule, and, in general, deal with an even greater hassle than before. He wanted something simple and effective. So Joel thought, "Well, I'll just create a better way to share on Twitter myself." And he did.

Buffer is an application that allows users to easily and efficiently share posts via social media by adding articles and multimedia to their account and then automatically posting throughout each day. It solves a single consumer problem— ease of sharing—and focuses on that problem alone. There's no stream or other features that are typically found in social media dashboards. "There are a lot of great solutions out there," Leo Widrich, head of community and coverage at Buffer, told me. "We picked just one that really needed improvement and focused solely on that."

The app is intuitive. After Buffer was launched in December 2010, people started paying for it in just three days, a sure sign of how useful users found it to be. It takes approximately one minute to get started with Buffer. This extremely low barrier to entry ensures an influx of sign-ups for the company as well as a simple user experience for consumers.

Having such a straightforward tool has helped the company itself become more focused. If your product has 10 core features, you might be unable to tell for sure which one solves the biggest problem for your customers and thus which is the most valuable. By focusing on just one feature, Buffer is able to better understand its customers and optimize the solution it provides. The company is able to then design a simple pricing strategy focusing on the core feature and offering upgrades with extra benefits customers may want. "Never letting go of this focus," Leo says, "is the key that we can keep Buffer super simple, intuitive, and useful at the same time." With its focus on simplicity, Buffer has reached 170,000 users and continues to grow 30 percent each month. (See Figure 10.1.)

What can businesses learn from Buffer? Determine the biggest problem you're solving for customers and cut out everything

FIGURE 10.1   **The team at Buffer keeps it simple.**
Source: Leo Widrich

that doesn't contribute to solving that one problem. Don't clutter your simple solution with unnecessary add-ons. Deliver an intuitive, consumer-focused product or service that simplifies, rather than complicates, your customers' lives.

WHY SIMPLE WORKS

Every organism right down to the amoeba is naturally inclined to seek the simplest solution to any problem, the simplest path from point A to point B. A Harvard University student conducted an experiment to determine if the simplest explanation for a cause would be chosen over more complex explanations. Subjects preferred the simpler explanation 100 percent of the time. Human beings crave simplicity.

Understanding this fact about human nature is key to delivering satisfaction to your customers. In an environment inundated with saturated product categories, cluttered advertising landscapes, and a constant influx of media, simplicity serves as a competitive advantage. In fact, consumers are 87 percent more likely to recommend to a friend a brand they consider simple versus a more complex one, according to new research conducted by *Marketing Week*. In an era when consumers are overwhelmed and confused by the insane amount of offerings, information, and messaging they receive on a daily basis from businesses and media, the perils of complexity are great. A study featured in the *Harvard Business Review* outlines the concept of the "decision simplicity index," a gauge of how easy it is for consumers to gather and understand information about a brand. The study uncovered three key factors: navigation (ease of gathering information), trust (how believable the information is), and comparison (ease of weighing options).[1] The easier you make it for consumers to decide, the more likely they are to choose you. And when you're not the simplest solution, you're guaranteed to lose out in the consumer decision-making process.

Before heading to Yahoo in the summer of 2012, Marissa Mayer was Google's director of consumer web products, and the company's heroine of simplicity. She understood how tapping into the human desire for simplicity has contributed to the company's success: "Google has the functionality of a really complicated Swiss Army knife," she has said, "but the home page is our way of approaching it closed. It's simple, it's elegant, you can slip it in your pocket, but it's got the great doodad when you need it. A lot of our competitors are like a Swiss Army knife open—and that can be intimidating and occasionally harmful." It's Google's uncomplicated design that has given the giant a majority share of the search market.

Google has mastered simplicity because it understands the way users behave and interact with products. When it comes to technology, consumers are seeking, above all, ease of use. Google gets it. Said Mayer, "[The Google home page] gives you what you want, when you want it, rather than everything you could ever want, even when you don't."[2] Consumers don't want everything they could possibly ever want; they want only what they want right now and nothing more.

Ron Ashkenas, managing partner of Schaffer Consulting and coauthor of *The GE Work-Out* and *The Boundaryless Organization*, describes his time with GE's consulting team in 1989. The team was formed by CEO Jack Welch to transform the company from slow and bureaucratic to fast and flexible. The team developed the "GE Work-Out process," with "simplicity" emerging as a key goal. In Welch's view, speed and simplicity were closely connected, and both were critical to the company's success. In order to move faster and be more responsive to customers and markets, GE would have to reduce the number of steps required to accomplish goals and make it easier for all employees to understand company processes. But simplicity at GE ultimately became more than just process streamlining—it became a company culture. It might seem radical to constantly think about how to become simpler and to embrace simplicity on every level, and yet it worked wonders for GE and it can work for you. For simplicity to succeed, it can't be just a marketing or an organization strategy, but rather an essential value and philosophy, reaching to every aspect of the business.

THINK APPLE

You can't talk about being simple without talking about Apple. The brand itself stands for simplicity, which is in its list of core values: "We believe in the simple, not the complex." Every aspect of the company, from products to operations to advertising, communicates simplicity (and does so simply). Just take a glance at an iPhone, which has only one button, the "home button" (see Figure 10.2). Why only one button? Because that's the simplest design for a phone. The design of the iPhone is not overthought; no Apple product is.

FIGURE 10.2   **Apple's iPhone is the epitome of simplicity.**
Source: Cliff Sebastian

SIMPLE COMMUNICATION

Simplicity involves knowing, without a doubt, who your company is, and communicating this information to others. Your customers' capacity to understand you is partly what allows them to trust you. Knowing who you are shouldn't be difficult for small companies, but as you grow, your risk of losing yourself grows too. Yet some big companies, such as Apple, are able to clearly articulate what their brand essence is, what their values are, and what they stand for. When we ask a question, we don't want a roundabout, difficult, fluff-filled response; we want the straightforward answer. And we expect the same from businesses. Consumers need to be able to understand, without confusion or superfluousness, who you are, what you do, and what your products or services do.

Apple didn't introduce the iPod to consumers as "a 6.5-ounce music player with a 5-gigabyte drive." The iPod was described as "1,000 songs in your pocket." This is the way consumers communicate with one another, and so that's how Apple communicates with consumers. "Human-speak is a hallmark of simplicity," says Ken Segall, former ad agency creative director for Apple.[3] This means using clarity in communication and speaking in simple, human terms.

BEHAVE SIMPLY

Apple models itself as "a small group of smart people." It's a big company that acts like a start-up. "We're the biggest start-up on the planet," Steve Jobs once said. "I don't see why you have to change as you get big."[4] I do. As a company grows, simple behavior becomes harder to scale, with complex processes and large groups of (sometimes) smart people becoming the norm. So how do you keep thinking like a start-up along the way to becoming a Fortune 500 company? You stay ruthlessly committed.

And Steve Jobs was. In *Insanely Simple: The Obsession That Drives Apple's Success*, Ken Segall recounts a time when Jobs threw a woman out of a meeting: "He stopped cold. His eyes locked onto the one thing in the room that didn't look right. Pointing to Lorrie, he said, 'Who are you?'" After her reply, Jobs then "hit her with the Simple Stick," saying "I don't think we need you in this meeting, Lorrie. Thanks." Why did he send her away? Simply because she wasn't necessary.

Simplicity doesn't require rudeness or maliciousness, but the fact of the matter is, every person at your company should be valuable and necessary, and so should every person at every meeting. Everyone must serve a purpose.

RUTHLESSLY SIMPLIFY

As Steve Jobs proved, simplicity isn't something that can be just added to a company; it needs someone to guide and to stubbornly champion it. This person doesn't have to be the CEO, but it needs to be someone. And simplicity must be implemented with consistency, until it is simply part of the company itself. The champion of simplicity must have the determination to hold fast to his or her mission and not allow others to complicate simple things. Simplicity, frankly, must be fought for.

But it's worth it. Literally.

SIMPLICITY DELIVERS

The size of Apple's profits compared with those of the competition in the first quarter of 2012 proves the power of simplicity. Apple's quarterly revenue of $46.33 billion beat out Google, was double that of Microsoft's, and, according to *Wall Street Journal*'s Scott Austin, exceeded the GDP of 105 countries. In the first quarter, Apple sold 5.2 million Macs, representing a 26 percent growth rate in a declining market.[5]

Simplicity is what drives Apple to create the products and develop the behavior required to produce these astounding business results.

SIMPLICITY MAKES IT EASIER
FOR PEOPLE TO HELP YOU

When I had the pleasure of chatting with Verne Harnish, the founder of Entrepreneurs Organization and author of *Mastering the Rockefeller Habits*, we discussed the principle of simplicity. At first, Verne wasn't getting where I was going with simplicity, especially with regard to traditional businesses, for whom simplicity in Internet or app design isn't relevant.

Then he said, "I'll tell you one thing: The more simple your ask of people is, the easier it is for people to help you."

A lightbulb lit up for me when Verne said that. I had spent months forming a really strong advisory board, seasoned professionals whom my wife and I could turn to for help growing our company. And yet at our first meeting, I wasn't sure we accomplished all that much. I expected these heavy hitters to have nonstop ideas, referrals, and help. But I had shared too much, asked too much, and had too many focuses.

With so many focuses, I had no focus. I followed up the advisory board meeting with one simple request for help via e-mail: "Can you speak at our upcoming Likeable U conference or recommend someone who can?" All 11 people responded right away and helped.

FOCUS ON THE FEW

It's not as easy to simplify as it is to start out simple, but it's not impossible. Unilever is a prime example of the power and possibility of simplification. Following acquisitions in the second half of the twentieth century, the company became bloated, with over 1200 brands in its portfolio. Unilever was suffering the downside of its giant size and scope: senior management had difficulty focusing, logistics were slow and inefficient, and decision making was complicated. The company determined a bold goal of cutting its portfolio while in return increasing its revenue and profits. To do this, it identified the small number of brands with the greatest growth potential and then focused efforts and strategy solely on those gems. Though it seemed absurdly implausible, Unilever was actually able to reduce its number of brands by a whopping 75 percent, yet boost sales. Start saying no to the underachieving business units, the irrelevant brand strategies, the useless product features, and start optimizing the viable ones. Focus on a few core competencies and forget about the rest.

FINDING YOUR ONE THING

Focus is imperative to simplicity. One of Apple's greatest strengths is its purity of purpose. The company focuses only on the products it makes well and refuses to be distracted by anything else. Apple isn't interested in attempting to please everyone.

As Steve Jobs once said, "People think focus means saying yes to the thing you've got to focus on. But that's not what it means at all. It means saying no to the hundred other good ideas that there are. You have to pick carefully. I'm actually as proud of the things we haven't done as the things we have done. Innovation is saying no to a thousand things."[6]

In fact, simplifying the Apple product line is what once saved the company. After his return to Apple in 1997, Steve Jobs reviewed the company's complex product line, which was filled with an overwhelming number of choices, and devised a simple chart representing a new product strategy. This diagram showed four quadrants: laptops for consumers, laptops for professionals, desktops for consumers, and desktops for professionals. That's it. With a simple chart, Steve Jobs readjusted Apple's focus and ultimately saved the company millions of dollars.

It's tempting for companies to try to be something to everyone and to accept every business opportunity that arises. However, success more often comes from electing to do only one thing and doing that one thing incredibly well; being the best. Apple has built a large and loyal fan base not because of the products it *can* make but because of the products it *decides* to make. As Steve Jobs once so eloquently put it, "Just get rid of the crappy stuff and focus on the good stuff."[7]

SIMPLE IS WORTH $1 BILLION

Instagram provides another great example of the value of simplicity. In the past year, Instagram attracted more than 80 million users, more than 1 billion uploaded photos, and $50 million in investments, including money from Twitter founder Jack Dorsey. Instagram has been successful because it asks users to just do one simple thing: share a photo. And it does that one thing flawlessly, even as the company has grown. "The best feature [of Instagram] is that it works," says cofounder Kevin Systrom. "We've been very careful about scaling. To be at 15 million users on one platform is not something any other social mobile company can say. There are a lot of others that are in that size range but are multi-platform. We saw an opportunity to be really good at one thing, and it turns out that helped us."[8]

In April 2012, Instagram's philosophy paid off to the tune of $1 billion in a deal with Facebook. Facebook's user experience was described by *New York Magazine* as "an NYPD police van crashing into an IKEA, forever—a chaotic mess of products designed to burrow into every facet of your life."[9] Facebook offers countless features and products, resembling the scattered Apple product line prior to the return of Jobs. So the social networking giant bought a company that does just one thing and does it extremely well to better solve a need of its users. If Instagram weren't so great at what it did, and if it didn't have just one singular product, it would never have been eyed by Facebook.

Don't be like the actor who decides to rap, and then launch a fashion line and a fragrance, and, oh yeah, model on the side. Figure out what you do best, and focus on that one thing. Without extreme targeting, you will dilute your mission and hinder your success. As Ron Swanson from the NBC show *Parks and Recreation* advises his coworker, "Never half ass two things. Whole ass one thing."

LIKEABLE SIMPLIFYING

The first few years of our company, we tried to be too many things to too many people. We were a "full-service social media leveraging and word-of-mouth marketing firm serving businesses, organizations, and governments large and small." Even the description sounds like the antithesis of simplicity. Our lack of clarity or simplicity led to decreased focus and to prospects and customers who wanted more than we could give them or had expectations different from ours. What we did and didn't do was often confusing—to customers, prospects, and even staff.

We had to simplify, if only for our own sanity. We thought about what we did best and for whom, and we relaunched with a focus on social content creation and community management for large brands. We were worried that our narrower focus and simplicity would alienate clients who had come to expect "full service." But the truth is, almost all of them appreciated our honesty about what we did best—and didn't do best. Our new simplicity led to us turning away some business, but it also led to clearer focus internally and externally, and our company continued rapid growth.

When we launched the Likeable Local platform for small businesses, every developer I talked to wanted to add in feature after feature to make the platform more useful and comprehensive. *The thing is, being comprehensive often flies in the face of being simple, and people crave simple.* So we resisted all the added features and benefits and built a social media marketing platform for small business that included only the basics: Facebook content, apps, and ads. Was I afraid that this wasn't enough? Absolutely terrified. But I'd rather start simple and add things later than start too complex and have people not get it and give up trying.

THE NEGATIVE OF BEING
ALL THINGS TO ALL PEOPLE

BlackBerry once enjoyed great popularity among businesses, in part for its commitment to security. But in the wake of the consumer market's love affair with smartphones, Research In Motion (RIM), the company that produces BlackBerry, sought a bigger piece of the pie, positioning its products as both consumer and business goods.

This move turned out to be a misstep for the company. BlackBerry failed to compete with the more lusted-after and consumer-oriented Apple and Android models, and efforts to produce a tablet competitor to the iPad flopped. In December 2011, RIM's PlayBook was selling below the cost of production.

In March 2012, after quarterly results fell short of Wall Street expectations, the company announced a return to focus. "We believe that BlackBerry cannot succeed if we try to be everybody's darling and all things to all people," said CEO Thorsten Heins. "Therefore, we plan to build on our strength."[10]

RIM reported a net loss of $125 million, or 24 cents a share, in the first quarter of 2012, compared with profits of $934 million, or $1.78 per share, the previous year. Revenue fell 25 percent to $4.2 billion from $5.6 billion, while analysts were expecting a revenue of $4.5 billion.

Concluded Heins, "We can't do everything ourselves, but we can do what we're good at."

When you start trying to solve every problem, serve every niche, and take advantage of every opportunity, you lose focus, lose sight of who you are, and ultimately lose to competitors. Stick to what you're good at.

KEEP IT SIMPLE STUPID

The adage "Keep it simple stupid" was coined by a lead engineer at Lockheed Martin who presented a team of design engineers with a handful of tools and a challenge: a jet aircraft must be repairable by (a) an average mechanic in the field, (b) under combat conditions, and (c) with these tools alone. The "stupid" referred not to the engineers (as in "Keep it simple, stupid"), but to the relationship between the way things break and the tools available to fix them (as in "Keep it simple stupid"). Don't overthink any aspect of your business. The tools to solve any business problem should already be available; they are simple, as the solutions must be.

When Intuit developed its small-business accounting software package, developers realized that most small-business owners were confused and intimidated by accounting jargon. So they decided to call "accounts receivable" "money in" and "accounts payable" "money out." Because its developers created a product from the customer perspective, Intuit sold 100,000 copies of the software the first year. Stick to the basics, and keep it simple stupid.

SIMPLICITY: SOCIAL TOOLS AND PRINCIPLES

Not every social media channel is right for you and your audience. Companies have a tendency to get overexcited when they get involved with social networks, but the truth is, often one or two social networks is enough, especially when you're just getting started and don't yet fully understand which social networks your customers are spending their time on. Keep your social media marketing plan simple! There's no need to set up profiles on Pinterest, Google+, or Twitter if your audience is primarily using Facebook and LinkedIn. Integrate social campaigns into your marketing and your customers' lives without overcomplicating them. We can also learn a lot from the design simplicity inherent in some of the world's most popular social tools. Twitter, Instagram, Quora, and Pinterest are all supersimple. So when you're designing a Facebook application or online question-and-answer forum or any proprietary social tool for your business, keep it simple! Just make it work and make it add value. That's really all your customers want.

ACTION ITEMS

1. Write down your company's core values. Be able to articulate who you are as a company, in the simplest terms, to your employees and customers.
2. Write down in the simplest form possible what you do, in no more than 140 characters. This is how simply you should be able to express yourself to your audience.

FIGURE 11.2   The Dave Kerpen Building stands as a testament to the power of gratitude.
Source: Carrie Kerpen

And do you think I will want to continue to help my friend however I can? Of course! Gratefulness and kindness form a virtuous circle, and more often than not, being thankful and doing good not only make us feel good; they make amazing things happen in our businesses and our lives.

YOU GET WHAT YOU GIVE

Verne Harnish, founder of the Young Entrepreneurs' Organization (now the Entrepreneurs' Organization) and founder of Gazelles, Inc., was once advised that if he were ever in financial trouble, he should go out and make a significant donation in order to get the money flowing again. After

3. Figure out what you do best. Start by asking your customers and employees what their favorite aspect of your company is. Then focus on just that one thing.

4. Hit your company with the "simple stick" wherever you can. Ask yourself, "What's unnecessary? What can we get rid of? How can we make this simpler?"

5. Identify a champion of simplicity at your company. Who is your Marissa Mayer or your Steve Jobs? If you don't have one, step into that role.

6. Make simplicity part of your corporate culture. Otherwise, it's ineffective, just for show, and not a true value of your company.

BE SIMPLY HUMAN

Simplicity involves, in essence, being human. You must never lose sight of the basics or stray from the human level. You can't master simplicity without fully understanding human behavior. Your company must listen to its customers and then create the intuitive, easy-to-use products and services that will satisfy just what they need (and nothing more).

CHAPTER 11

Gratefulness
The ROI of "Thank You"

I would maintain that thanks are the highest form of thought, and
that gratitude is happiness doubled by wonder.

—Gilbert K. Chesterton

Nora Firestone had always said she wished she could one day go
back and thank every single teacher who has made a difference
in her life. So one day, she did just that. She decided it was time
to track down and contact each former teacher of hers. Over the
course of two years, using many different methods of searching,
Nora finally found and thanked every teacher who has had an
impact on her life.

Her sixth-grade gym teacher, Mr. Sybil, had been especially
significant. Nora recalls a time when she raced against her
grade's rope-climbing champ, the "toughest girl" at John H. West
Elementary School in 1977. Struggling to keep up, Nora looked
to Mr. Sybil, whose intense eyes were locked on her as he quietly
chanted, "You can do it! Hang in there! You can do it! Hang in
there!" Suddenly, the calls of surrounding naysayers faded away,
and Nora focused on the one person in the room who knew her

like she knew herself, a man who believed fully in her potential. That moment changed Nora's life for the better, teaching her determination, and she's been incredibly grateful for Mr. Sybil's support ever since.

When she found her gym teacher years later, he was retired and dealing with a medical disability. Nora thanked him for helping to shape and strengthen her during that critical time in her life and reminded him of what he once told her: "You can do it! Hang in there!" Being reminded of that moment and hearing her gratitude allowed Mr. Sybil to summon his own strength, showing that what goes around sometimes does come back around.

This experience was so wonderful that it made Nora stop and think: What if she could help others express their gratefulness too? So Nora created ThankingOfYou.com, a website that helps people track down and thank individuals who have made a difference in their lives.

"What I have been doing is a lot of promoting the virtue," she said to me. "I feel like I've already benefited so much in my lifetime by focusing on the gifts that I've been given."

She often receives thank you notes of her own from gracious users of ThankingOfYou.com. One particular user, Sheila, was finally able to put 30+ years of gratitude for her former high school teacher Mrs. Stafford on paper, after years of unsuccessful searching. Finding the words that expressed her sincere appreciation filled Sheila's heart with joy.

Nora explains the incredible impact that gratefulness has had on her life: by focusing on gratefulness, she's become a much happier person. She lives by the philosophy that expressing gratefulness, even for something very small, can have a great impact on a person.

After creating the site, Nora let Mr. Sybil know that her experience with him inspired the creation of ThankingOfYou.com. Mr. Sybil now calls Nora several times a year, and she has visited him in person while visiting family on Long Island. Nora doesn't just practice gratefulness in her everyday life; she built a business on it.

THE INCREDIBLE POWER
OF GRATEFULNESS

People who start powerful movements to better the world tend to first recognize and be grateful for something in their own lives. In order to bring good to someone else's life, you must be able to understand the good in your own.

While participating in the *Amazing Race,* Blake Mycoskie stopped in Argentina, where he witnessed extreme poverty and poor health conditions as well as numerous children walking around without shoes. This experience led him to start his company, TOMS Shoes, and its One for One program: for each pair of shoes sold, Blake donates a pair to a child in need. The goal of TOMS is to show how, by working together, we can create a better tomorrow by doing a good deed and being compassionate today. "I was so overwhelmed by the spirit of the South American people, especially those that had so little," Blake says. "And I was instantly struck with the desire—the responsibility—to do more."[1] During its first year in business, TOMS sold 10,000 pairs of shoes. Blake returned to Argentina a year after the company launched to give back to the children who had inspired him. Following a business strategy revolving around gratitude and giving, TOMS has sold over 600,000 pairs of shoes to date. By recognizing the good in their lives, Blake, TOMS customers, and supporters have been able to pass that good on to others.

Any great company, organization, or movement comes from a place of someone's deepest sense of gratitude. We must nurture the aspects we value to bring more good to our lives, the lives of others, and our environments.

HOW PAYING IT FORWARD PAYS OFF

The business value of gratefulness is simply the act itself. The world is balanced: the more good you do, the more good there is in the world, the more good will come back to you. Positive energy attracts positive energy. It's not about "tit for tat" and reciprocity; it's about doing the right thing, being gracious and thankful, no matter the rewards.

But there will be rewards, of course, the first of which are happiness and positivity. Studies show that those who frequently feel and express gratefulness often have more energy, more optimism, more social connections, and more joy than those who don't.[2] Thankful individuals also experience far less depression, envy, and greed; they earn more money, sleep more restfully, and are overall healthier spiritually, mentally, and physically. Being grateful also allows you to overcome a "negativity bias," the innate tendency to dwell on problems and negative points rather than solutions and positive points. Focusing on the good can foster resilience.

Cary Chessick is the former CEO of Restaurant.com, a website that gives customers deals at their favorite restaurants, and now the CEO of Score It Forward, a consulting organization with the mission to put a soccer ball in the hands of every child. More important to me, he's a friend who has truly taught me the value of gratitude. For Cary, gratitude is a core tenet of positive psychology that he shared with his team. "Gratitude is a rarity," Cary said to me. "It's something everyone knows they should do, but they don't. It's a niche."

When Cary decided to make gratitude a core value of his company, he started with a campaign called "Feed It Forward," allowing participants to give $10 gift certificates for free from the site's stock of 4 million certificates totaling $40 million. Looking back on the campaign, Cary says, the most striking element was not the program itself but the feedback from the community of givers and the thank you notes and responses from employees: "There was a whirlwind of gratitude flowing out from so many people across the company, stranger to stranger to stranger, that ultimately led us to evolve the program to include random acts of kindness."

Ever since that campaign, Cary has believed in creating a pay-it-forward society and inspiring gratitude. Cary himself has made it a point to write thank you notes to his employees, which he says are valuable because they bring a meaningfulness to his employees' work and make them feel better about themselves. "If you love your job and you think your work is meaningful, you're more likely to be productive," says Cary. "If you think your job doesn't have a lot of meaning, you're less likely to be happy, and if you're unhappy, then you're more likely to be unproductive." Cary says that his employees come into work with a bounce in their step, knowing they'll be able to help someone that day.

It's trite but true: what goes around comes around. Think about it as business karma. If you make it a practice to genuinely thank those who deserve your thanks, they will appreciate your expression of gratitude and will be far more willing to help you out when you need their assistance.

DONORS CHOOSE AND THE ROI OF GRATITUDE

Charles Best is the founder and CEO of Donors Choose, an online nonprofit organization that makes it easy for donors to give to classrooms in need. Donors literally choose classroom projects they want to fund and then donate to make those projects come alive.

Charles shared with me a study he conducted to demonstrate the ROI (return on investment) of gratitude. In this experiment, the Donors Choose staff sent handwritten thank you notes to half of their recent first-time donors. The results showed a direct correlation between the act of being thanked and the likelihood of giving again. In fact, those who were personally thanked were 38 percent more likely to give another donation, proving an actual ROI of gratitude (see Figure 11.1).

Expressing gratitude and saying thank you personally are an essential part of the Donors Choose business model. When donors are compelled to give money, for whom do they open their wallets? The organization that appreciates their gift and sends a handwritten note. As Charles said to me, "The offline component has made our organization an online success." Donors Choose does more than give money to classrooms; it encourages and inspires an entire culture and movement of gratefulness. After projects are successfully funded by Donors

THE R.O.I OF
THANK-YOU NOTES

	TEST GROUP	CONTROL GROUP
	THANK-YOU NOTE MAILED EARLY FEBRUARY	DID NOT RECEIVE THANK-YOU NOTE
NEW DONORS DONATED $100 - $999 BETWEEN 7/1/11 AND 2/1/12	879	857
DONATED AGAIN BETWEEN 2/1/12 AND 5/21/12	105	74
% DONATING AGAIN	11.95	8.63
AVERAGE DONATION SIZE OF THOSE WHO GAVE AGAIN	$232.09	$231.74

FIGURE 11.1 **Donors were 38 percent more likely to give again after being personally thanked.**
Source: Donors Choose and Ramon Thompson

Choose, teachers and their students send thank you notes to donors, and donors often end up sending thank you notes back to the classrooms for taking the time to send a thank you! One thank you leads to an endless cycle of gratitude. It's the principle of "paying it forward" at its best.

THE EO EXPERIENCE AND HOW GRATEFULNESS ALWAYS PAYS ITSELF BACK

Two years ago, I joined the Entrepreneurs' Organization. EO is a global network of CEOs and founders of companies with annual revenues of $1 million or more. Many of EO's 8,500 members and members of its sister organization, Young Presidents Organization, run companies making a lot more—as much as $50 million a year or more. When I joined EO, I was afraid I was getting into a club of rich, selfish people out of touch with their employees and the world.

As it turned out, that fear couldn't have been more unfounded. In the two years that I've been in EO, I've met hundreds of amazing, giving individuals in my New York chapter and around the world. I've learned immeasurable things about business and life from fellow members and inspirational speakers at events, such as Lauren Bush, Warren Rustand, Carl Gould, and Meg Hirshberg. EO reminds us to be thankful for what we have and to give back to each other and to the world—to give not in order to receive but because it's the right thing to do.

As much as I've treasured my EO experience, I wasn't sure whether I should write about it in this book. But I kept coming back to how grateful I am for EO. To not write about my EO experience in this chapter would be doing a disservice to any reader who might qualify to join.

One of my favorite experiences in EO has been coaching forum members in presentations. Each month, a small group of members gets together, and the nine of us talk about our businesses and lives. One person gives a presentation about something deeply meaningful in his or her life, and another coaches him or her to get the most value out of the presentation.

A year ago, I coached my friend Andy on a presentation about gratitude and acts of kindness. He wanted to operationalize these things—to systematically make sure he has been grateful and kind each day, with the simple goal of living a better life.

We devised a plan, and Andy began writing three thank you notes a day and performing three random acts of kindness a day. Word caught on, and others in the forum began doing the same. We did this not for what we expected to get back but simply because it felt good to be grateful. I worked my butt off for Andy not because I expected anything but because it felt good to help.

Now it just so happens that my friend is in real estate, and his company owns several buildings. A year later I got a phone call from Andy: "Dave, I'm so grateful for you. I'd like to name a building after you." I don't know what the ROI is of having a building named after you, and I don't care. In June 2012, the Dave Kerpen Building (see Figure 11.2) went up in Newark, New Jersey, and now I am eternally grateful to Andy and his thoughtfulness.

September 11, 2001, Harnish found himself in such a financial situation, at risk of losing both his house and his company. That fall, his church was conducting its largest fund-raising campaign, asking for a three-year commitment. So Harnish went to his wife and suggested they contribute. After making the largest donation he had ever made in his life, Harnish netted 10 times the amount of that donation the next year. In fact, each time he makes a monetary contribution, he gains 10 times the amount back. Harnish has learned an incredibly valuable lesson: you must give before you can receive. In business, you truly do reap what you sow.

UNDERSTANDING WHO AND WHAT HAVE LED TO YOUR SUCCESS

On Thanksgiving Day 2010, General Motors ran an ad entitled "We all fall down . . . Thank you for helping us get back up." The ad included images of boxers, Evel Knievel, and Harry Truman, taking viewers through a sentimental series of triumphs and defeats and ending with GM's expression of gratitude. GM's message focused solely on saying thank you—no sales pitch, no product features. Jeff Goodby, cochairman of GM's ad agency, Goodby, Silverstein & Partners, admitted that GM and his team contemplated alternatives but then GM realized, "It's not about us."[3] It was about the customers, the people who contributed to GM's comeback. GM knew that the ad likely wouldn't sell more cars, but the company recognized that it could positively impact its corporate reputation and express to the public how humble and thankful GM had become.

Being grateful for what you have requires reflecting on those who have helped you along the way. By thanking them, you consciously acknowledge what has contributed to your success; and by understanding what has influenced you and your business, you're able to continue that success—those influential people will continue to assist you, and you'll simultaneously do more of the good you've done in the past.

THANK YOUR CUSTOMERS AND CLIENTS

On April 17, 2012, Cinnabon launched a campaign called "Tax Day Bites," during which everyone who visited a Cinnabon location was entitled to two free Cinnabon minis. On the same day, Cinnabon released a YouTube video entitled "Cinnabon's Tribute to Our Followers on Tax Day." The caption for the video read "We have the best fans and Twitter followers in the world. This year on Tax Day, we wanted to make a video to recognize you." The video itself starts out by asking, "Why are we giving away two free minis on Tax Day?" and then shows screenshots of tweets from followers along with fun, silly reasons that Cinnabon loves its fans, such as "because you put us in the same category as McDreamy" and "because we're part of your 'strict' diet." Cinnabon didn't require its customers to bring in a coupon or voucher to receive free minis. Instead, the company made it as easy as possible for its fans to get their hands on some free sweet treats. This was a brilliant move by Cinnabon, because not only do people love getting free stuff, but they also love talking about getting free stuff.

When you thank people and show your gratitude, they know they're valued and feel honored to be acknowledged. They are then excited to talk about you and are sure to continue to do business with you.

One of my employees, Brian Murray, recently used the services of Intern Sushi after the start-up reached out to him. The company helps interns find positions and helps companies find applicants by giving them a platform to share their stories via video. Intern Sushi encourages users to be as picky about their internships as they are about their sushi. Brian was particularly enthusiastic about and appreciative of the company, and the company was just as thrilled about and grateful for him. The company surprised Brian with a gift of candy sushi and a handwritten note, thoroughly thanking him for using the service (see Figure 11.3). Says Brian, "After e-mails and phone calls, a simple thank you note and candy made me fall in love with them. I will never forget the moment I realized someone took the time out of their day to write me a personalized note."

FIGURE 11.3 **Intern Sushi's little thank you note made a huge statement.**
Source: Theresa Braun

The team at Guidant Financial is particularly dedicated to showing clients, without the use of a social media megaphone, that it cares about them and appreciates them. Every month, the team at Guidant Financial narrows down its client list to the top three and then votes on the Client of the Month. The entire team then signs an enormous three-foot card and presents it to the client. Why?

"We wanted to connect our staff with our clients," David Nilssen, CEO of Guidant Financial, told me. "It's so easy to get muddled in the details and forget the little things. We want to keep an ongoing relationship with our clients and make them aware that we appreciate them."

Going the extra mile to surprise clients with enormous cards and staff visits has certainly been worthwhile for Guidant Financial. A whopping 20 percent of Guidant Financial's business comes from client referrals. That means that a fifth of Guidant Financial's revenue comes from the team telling its clients "thank you" every once in a while.

THANK YOU NOTES, **NOT** E-MAILS, MAKE A DIFFERENCE

Though I thought I had been practicing gratitude in our business by constantly thanking staff and customers via e-mail, an e-mail "thank you" is just not that special these days. E-mails are supereasy to write and send; and while some people may appreciate receiving them, others may actually resent you for further cluttering their inbox. I learned from Cary Chessick to write personalized thank you notes. For several years now, Cary has begun each day by writing five thank you notes to people in his business and life. I started slower than that, to better ensure I'd deliver against my goal.

I began by writing three personalized thank you notes each Wednesday and then increased to three thank you notes each weekday. I also asked our management team to do the same, one day each week. The experiment proved powerful very quickly. Some recipients of our thank you notes were moved to tears, some just to nice tweets. But everyone appreciated the extra time it took to handwrite a thank you card, seal it, and deliver or send it. In an increasingly digital world, there's something magical about receiving a handwritten note.

My hope and expectation is that thank you cards will help build loyalty and pride both among our team and with our customers. But no matter what, it feels darn good to write them and send them.

Thanking employees leads to productivity and loyalty within a company. If employees feel that their managers are genuinely grateful for the work they contribute, they are far happier and more productive as a result. If you know your work is valued, you're much more likely to continue to do it and do it well.

THANK YOUR FAMILY, FRIENDS, AND MENTORS

No one can rise to greatness on his or her own. Success isn't achieved in a vacuum. Each of us has a parent, teacher, or friend who has influenced us, taught us, pushed us, inspired us to be great, to work hard, to achieve something amazing.

Imagine your life without that person. Try the *It's a Wonderful Life* test: how would your life and your accomplishments be affected by the absence of that significant, influential person? Acknowledging those who have touched your life—from the barista who makes your coffee each morning to your middle school math teacher—and reflecting on how you can reciprocate will foster humbleness and an understanding of our world's interdependence. You can't build a successful company without at least a little support. So don't forget to thank those that have helped you along the way.

A CORPORATE CULTURE OF GRATEFULNESS

Andy Cohen is the founder and CEO of Rock Properties, a real estate investment company in New York, New Jersey, and Connecticut. The Rock Properties team is motivated by inspiring its neighbors and being conscious of the fact that housing is among a person's most basic needs. The members of the Rock Properties team believe their job is not only to provide housing but also to perform acts of kindness. The leadership and employees alike at Rock Properties operate under the mentality that gratefulness has an impact within the company. Each day, the leaders at Rock Properties make it a point to do three good deeds and send e-mails for five different things they're grateful for at the moment. The idea is that if they continue to focus on the positive things they've been given, they'll be able to focus on the positive in other areas as well, leading to a greater overall sense of happiness.

Gratitude, if incorporated into your company's culture, can have an incredible impact on your business. Thank yous can be a productivity tool, affecting how well your team works together. Gratefulness allows employees to recognize their interdependence and need for each other, leading to greater teamwork. Gratitude's focus on what's good or important fosters creativity and cooperation. People with negative attitudes focus on flaws and the things that are wrong with their day, but people with positivity find the good in every person and situation and are more motivated to do their work. Gratitude fosters intellectual and emotional tools like resourcefulness and resilience, creating better team members.

LOOK FOR THE WONDER IN THE WORLD

Mike Maddock, founder and CEO of Maddock Douglas, Inc., tells the story of two shoe salesmen who travel to Asia in search of potential buyers. One day, their manager calls to check in. "How's it going?" he asks. The first salesman replies, "Terrible, no one wears any shoes here!" The second salesman replies, "Great, everyone needs shoes here!" In business, there will always be roadblocks, mistakes, and misfortune. The difference between a successful business leader and a failure is whether you see challenges as stumbling blocks or opportunities. It all comes down to being grateful for challenges.

Mike recounted to me a time when his company lost 45 percent of its business in the span of three months. Most companies that lose that much business are goners within a year. But Mike recognized this "punch in the face" as a wake-up call and an opportunity to implement a change in the company. Looking at the situation as "half full," Mike realized there was good news: the company was currently addressing a white space in the industry by helping businesses with innovation, figuring out the answer to "What's next?" So Maddock Douglas became an "Agency of Innovation" and for the last 20 years has been prompting clients like Walmart, GE, and Kraft to invent new products, services, and strategies.

Had it not been for Mike's positivity and optimism, his company likely would have shipwrecked. As Einstein once said, "The most important question for a human being to ask is, 'Is the universe friendly?'" If you see the universe as friendly, if you can detect wonder in the world, positivity and possibility will be infinitely more accessible.

On every vacation, Mike takes his kids on a treasure hunt, teaching them to constantly be on the lookout for wonder and appreciate the joy in life. Let there be no negativity in your company's culture. Those who can see the world as half full will be the producers of great work—hire the treasure-hunting wonder-seekers. Gratitude requires an appreciation for each situation and experience, a capacity to see the good amid misfortune.

There's treasure—unforeseen opportunity—in every job, every relationship, and every business situation. Those who find it are the ones who know to look for it. By having an appreciation for life, you will be able to focus on what matters most, be more joyous, and be readily receptive to new opportunities. Approach every business situation looking for the treasure.

UNGRATEFULNESS: DON'T BE THE JERK

Paige Arnof-Fenn, founder and CEO of strategic marketing and consulting firm Mavens and Moguls, was dealing with a bad client. He was unimpressed by the high-profile press her PR team had managed to land, and he was constantly late on payments. "I'll pay you when I pay you," he would say. There was no denying that this guy was a jerk, but Mavens and Moguls had just started out, and the client had signed a yearlong contract. So as protocol dictated, Paige rounded up her team and headed to the third monthly meeting with the client they dubbed "the Jerk." They all sat down together, talking about the work they'd done and highlighting the stellar press the PR team had generated. The Jerk was unimpressed by the work they'd done, save for an appearance in his local, small-town newspaper that he said made him feel like a celebrity because he was recognized when he went to the dry cleaners.

After Paige's team wrapped up their presentation, Paige asked the Jerk if he'd like to thank the team for their hard work. They had been working long hours for about half the pay they deserved. "Thank you?" the Jerk asked, as if Paige had suggested something completely outrageous. "Why would I thank you? I *hired* you! Isn't that enough thanks?" At that point, Paige snapped. "You know," she said, "I think maybe we ought to just shake hands and part ways." "Are you *firing* me as a client?" asked the Jerk. "Yes," Paige answered. "I think I am."

Paige describes firing the Jerk as a defining moment for her company and her team. They had just started out, and this event set an important precedent. From then on, the Mavens and Moguls team became much more selective about which clients they worked with because, as Paige says, they "didn't want to be known for helping jerks." The moral of the story is a simple one: don't be a jerk. Recognize your team, your clients, and your customers for their accomplishments and contributions, big and small. People may be able to overlook a late payment, but no one will overlook someone who acts like an ungrateful jerk.

GRATEFULNESS: SOCIAL TOOLS AND PRINCIPLES

Social media allows for expressions of gratitude in business at greater scale than ever before possible. You might not be able to thank every person who has had a positive impact on your life, but you can certainly make a start by personally thanking everyone who gives feedback, retweets your content, or pays you a complimentary Facebook post. Also consider doing good deeds for your fans and followers. I often randomly ask my Twitter followers what I can retweet or do to help them out—as you can see in Figure 11.4. I don't do it to gain some-

Dave Kerpen
@DaveKerpen
Following
What can I RT to my 16k followers to help you right now? Share your links / tweets via @reply, I will RT all in next 4 minutes.
Reply
Retweet
Favorite

FIGURE 11.4 A simple tweet has great potential to give back to followers.

thing from them; I do it because I'm grateful for each and every one of them and want to give back.

Social tools also allow leaders to more efficiently express gratitude within an organization. Let's say you want to share a message of thanks with the entire company. You could send out a mass e-mail or printed letter, but that might be seen as formal and impersonal. Or you could record a short video to post within your closed company Facebook group. The video would allow you to better convey your sentiment, and employees could immediately share their own feedback, adding to a sense of teamwork and collaboration.

Finally, social media creates public spaces in which thankfulness can be passed on and paid forward. Take a look at movements such as Tweetsgiving, Tweet It Forward, and thankfulfor. Then consider starting your own gratefulness movement across social networks. You never know how those random acts of Twitter kindness will come back to you.

ACTION ITEMS

1. Write down 10 people and things you're grateful for in your life right now.
2. The next time you are about to send a thank you e-mail to a client or colleague, write a thank you note and mail it. Send thank you notes to 10 people in your life you're grateful for: customers, coworkers, employees, spouses, children, siblings, parents, friends, neighbors, etc. Commit yourself to writing a certain number of thank you notes daily or weekly. Begin with one per day to keep it manageable.

BE THANKFUL

Gratitude isn't as big a part of business as it should be. Just as you thank someone for lending a hand or giving you a special gift, make sure to thank those in your life who have contributed to your business success. That good deed will come back to you tenfold. Grateful people are always looking for the good, and a likeable business is a grateful business. The amazing thing about gratefulness and unselfishness is this: whether or not there's an immediate ROI or increase in business value, there's always an immediate result in *your happiness.*

How dare you settle for less when the world has made it so easy for you to be remarkable?

—Seth Godin

Being a likeable business isn't rocket science. In fact, I'd be the first person to admit that few if any of the ideas in this book are revolutionary, and most are actually quite intuitive. Yet somewhere along the road, many organizations that may have started out with the best of intentions become less likeable. The good news is, just about all individuals are inherently likeable. Your challenge is to help your organization become more likeable, one person and one idea at a time. And it begins with you.

IT'S JUST A COCKTAIL PARTY

The cocktail party analogy doesn't hold true for social media only; it holds true for all business—and life. Yes, it's true: social media, business, and life in general, as it turns out, aren't much more complicated than a cocktail party. The person at a cocktail party who listens, who tells great stories, who is responsive, authentic, passionate, and grateful, will be the hit of the party time after time and will derive the most value from the party. The person who's direct and transparent, who knows how it keep it simple and always has a surprise up his sleeve, is the one worth hanging around. The guy who can go with the flow (adapt) and knows how to behave in a group is the guy you'll want in your circle. That same person will also be successful in the giant cocktail party known as the business world. So when faced with a quick decision, large or small, ask yourself: "Would this be a winning decision at a cocktail party?" If the answer is a resounding yes, you're likely on to something. If you're not so sure, you may want to rethink your decision. Yes, it really is as simple as that.

Of course, in today's social media–driven world, perhaps business is more like a cocktail party on a reality television show than a private party, because the world is watching. And even those who are not watching have more access to watch than ever before, and they are probably just a click or two away from watching—watching and sharing your success or your failure, that is.

CHOOSE YOUR OWN LIKEABLE ADVENTURE

All the principles in this book might not readily apply to you and your organization. I'm hopeful that some of the stories triggered thoughts about how you might go about your business a bit differently. I sincerely hope that you found at least a few chapters to have some implications for your business and that now you can go back, review the action steps at the end of those chapters, and start doing the work of implementation.

THIS IS ACTUALLY THE BEGINNING

That's right—it's the end of the book but the beginning of your journey toward increased likeability and increased success. I'm so grateful to you for your purchase of this book and even more grateful for your most precious resource, your time in reading it. Thank you for spending your time with me and this book. I truly hope to demonstrate my gratefulness through my own responsiveness, so please do feel free to contact me to ask me any questions or share feedback, ideas, and struggles—now or for the rest of your life—on Twitter (@DaveKerpen), on Facebook (FB.com/LikeableBook), or via e-mail (dave@likeable.com). I promise to respond, and I hope I can help.

I can't wait to hear your stories of becoming more likeable and how it affects your bottom line. Your customers and colleagues deserve it. And you deserve it too.

The following is a list of recommended books to continue your exploration of the key concepts of a likeable business. Happy reading!

General Reads for Business Leaders

Great by Choice, by Jim Collins and Morten T. Hansen
The Four Obsessions of an Extraordinary Executive: A Leadership Fable, by Patrick Lencioni
Word of Mouth Marketing, by Andy Sernovitz
The Mesh, by Lisa Gansky
For Better or for Work: A Survival Guide for Entrepreneurs and Their Families, by Meg Cadoux Hirshberg
Tribes, by Seth Godin
Digital Leaders: 5 Simple Keys to Success and Influence, by Erik Qualman
Built to Sell, by John Warrilow
Running the Gauntlet, by Jeffrey Hayzlett
Uncertainty: Turning Fear and Doubt into Fuel for Brilliance, by Jonathan Fields
Launch, by Mike Steizner

Listening

Listen First! Turning Social Media Conversations into Business Advantage, by Stephen D. Rappaport
The Business of Listening, by Diana Bonet
Crucial Conversations: Tools for Talking When Stakes Are High, by Kerry Patterson
Power Listening: Mastering the Most Critical Business Skill of All, by Bernard T. Ferrari

Just Listen: Discover the Secret to Getting Through to Absolutely Anyone, by Mark Goulston

Storytelling

The Leader's Guide to Storytelling: Mastering the Art and Discipline of Business Narrative, by Stephen Denning

The Story Factor, by Annette Simmons

Whoever Tells the Best Story Wins: How to Use Your Own Stories to Communicate with Power and Impact, by Annette Simmons

Tell to Win: Connect, Persuade, and Triumph with the Hidden Power of Story, by Peter Guber

The Presentation Secrets of Steve Jobs: How to Be Insanely Great in Front of Any Audience, by Carmine Gallo

Authenticity

Authenticity: What Consumers Really Want, by James H. Gilmore

Sincerity and Authenticity, by Lionel Trilling

The Ethics of Authenticity, by Charles Taylor

On Being Authentic, by Charles B. Guignon

Transparency

Transparency: How Leaders Create a Culture of Candor, by Warren Bennis, Daniel Goleman, James O'Toole, and Patricia Ward Biederman

The Naked Corporation: How the Age of Transparency Will Revolutionize Business, by Don Tapscott

Tactical Transparency: How Leaders Can Leverage Social Media to Maximize Value and Build Their Brand, by Shel Holtz and John C. Havens

The Transparency Edge, by Barbara Pagano

Team Playing

Poke the Box, by Seth Godin

Good to Great: Why Some Companies Make the Leap . . . and Others Don't, by Jim Collins

Great Business Teams: Cracking the Code for Standout Performance, by Howard M. Guttman

The Secret of Teams: What Great Teams Know and Do, by Mark Miller and Ken Blanchard

Building Successful Teams, by Bill Butterworth

Free the Idea Monkey, by G. Michael Maddock

Responsiveness

United Breaks Guitars: The Power of One Voice in the Age of Social Media, by Dave Carroll

Enthusiasm Makes the Difference, by Norman Vincent Peale

Transforming Communication, Transforming Business: Building Responsive and Responsible Workplaces, by Stanley Deetz

The Power of Positive Thinking in Business, by Scott W. Ventrella

@Your Service: How to Attract New Customers, Increase Sales, and Grow Your Business Using Simple Customer Service Techniques, by Frank Eliason

Adaptability

The Lean Startup: How Today's Entrepreneurs Use Continuous Innovation to Create Radically Successful Businesses, by Eric Ries

Strategy and Business Process Management: Techniques for Improving Execution, Adaptability, and Consistency, by Carl F. Lehmann

The Power of Business Process Improvement: 10 Simple Steps to Increase Effectiveness, Efficiency, and Adaptability, by Susan Page

Adaptability: The Art of Winning in an Age of Uncertainty, by Max McKeown

Passion

Love the Work You're With: A Practical Guide to Finding New Joy and Productivity in Your Job, by Richard C. Whiteley

Accidental Branding: How Ordinary People Build Extraordinary Brands, by David Vinjamuri

Passion to Profits: Business Success for New Entrepreneurs, by Rhonda Abrams

Passion and Purpose: Stories from the Best and Brightest Young Business Leaders, by John Coleman

Delivering Happiness: A Path to Profits, Passion, and Purpose, by Tony Hsieh

Surprise and Delight

Be Our Guest: Perfecting the Art of Customer Service, by the Disney Institute

Uncommon Service: How to Win by Putting Customers at the Core of Your Business, by Frances Frei and Anne Morriss

Exceptional Experience: What the World's Most Famous (Former) Madam Can Teach You About Business, Customer Service, Employee Relations & Entrepreneurship, by Lori Webb

Exceptional Service, Exceptional Profit: The Secrets of Building a Five-Star Customer Service Organization, by Leonardo Inghilleri

The Customer Delight Principle: Exceeding Customers' Expectations for Bottom-Line Success, by Timothy L. Keiningham

Simplicity

Insanely Simple: The Obsession That Drives Apple's Success, by Ken Segall

Simplicity: The New Competitive Advantage in a World of More, Better, Faster, by Bill Jensen

The Laws of Simplicity, by John Maeda

Small Is the New Big, by Seth Godin

The Power of Simplicity, by Jack Trout

Gratefulness

Thanks! How the New Science of Gratitude Can Make You Happier, by Robert Emmons
The Thank You Economy, by Gary Vaynerchuck
Gratitude at Work: How to Say Thank You, Give Kudos, and Get the Best from Those You Lead, by April Kelly
Sacred Commerce, by Matthew Engelhart

Notes

INTRODUCTION

1. "Comcast's Twitter Man," *BusinessWeek*, http://www.businessweek .com/managing/content/jan2009/ca20090113_373506.htm.
2. http://simpliflying.com/2009/here-is-why-jetblue-is-the-most-loved -airline-brand-on-twitter/.
3. http://money.cnn.com/quote/financials/financials.html?symb= JBLU.

CHAPTER 1

1. http://www.nydailynews.com/life-style/better-boss-men-women -experts-females-tops-today-economy-article-1.431291.
2. http://blog.netflix.com/2011/10/dvds-will-be-staying-at-netflixcom .html.
3. http://money.cnn.com/2012/01/25/technology/netflix_earnings/ index.htm.
4. http://www.bellleadership.com/pressrelease/press_template.php?id =12.
5. http://www.bellleadership.com/pressreleases/press_template.php?id =12.
6. http://www.emarketer.com/blog/index.php/case-study-ibm-drives -millions-dollars-worth-sales-leads-social-media/.
7. http://www.drnatalienews.com/blog/could-social-media -monitoring-have-saved-netflix-blockbuster-from-themselves#.

CHAPTER 2

1. John Green, *An Abundance of Katherines*, Penguin, 2006, p. 202.
2. OceanSpray.com.

CHAPTER 3

1. http://www.fanniemae.com/portal/about-us/company-overview/ about-fm.html.
2. http://www.businessinsider.com/worstceosever/franklin-raines.
3. "Saving Starbucks' Soul," http://www.businessweek.com/magazine/ content/07_15/b4029070.htm.

4. "Food Fighter: Does Whole Foods' CEO Know What's Best for You?" http://www.newyorker.com/reporting/2010/01/04/100104fa_fact_paumgarten?mobify=0.

5. "Startup Lessons Learned from Warren Buffett," http://venturebeat.com/2010/04/13/startup-lessons-learned-from-warren-buffett/.

6. Being Vulnerable in the Era of the Real-Time Web, as told by Jeff Pulver at #140cuse, April 19, 2012.

7. "Bethenny Frankel's Skinnygirl Deal: The Numbers Still Hold Up," http://www.forbes.com/sites/meghancasserly/2011/10/13/bethenny-frankels-skinnygirl-deal-the-numbers-still-hold-up/.

CHAPTER 4

1. http://www.bloomberg.com/news/2012-06-14/microsoft-said-to-be-in-talks-to-acquire-yammer-social-network.html.

2. http://www.bgr.com/2012/01/27/new-rim-ceo-admits-apple-and-google-are-winning-says-change-is-coming/.

3. http://www.chron.com/business/energy/article/BP-falls-short-in-estimate-of-oil-spill-rate-1717231.php.

CHAPTER 5

1. http://www.nytimes.com/2011/10/16/business/dan-schneider-founder-of-sib-on-handling-employee-errors.html?pagewanted=all.

2. "Robot Bosses, Unlimited Vacation, and Other Brilliant Management Ideas from Evernote's CEO," http://www.good.is/post/robot-bosses-unlimited-vacation-and-other-brilliant-management-ideas-from-evernote-s-ceo/.

3. http://www.adobe.com/aboutadobe/pressroom/pdfs/Adobe_State_of_Create_Global_Benchmark_Study.pdf.

4. http://www.fastcompany.com/1827003/how-kayak-created-a-culture-of-innovation.

5. Seth Godin, *Poke the Box,* The Domino Project, 2011, Introduction.

6. "Threadless: The Do-First Work Ethic," http://the99percent.com/videos/6299/threadless-the-do-first-work-ethic.

7. Miguel Helft and Jessi Hempel, "Inside Facebook: How Does the Social Media Giant Really Work? Read This Story Before You Buy the Stock," *Fortune*, March 26, 2012.

8. http://www.convinceandconvert.com/brand-communities/threadless-shares-10-years-of-insights-and-inspiration.

9. "Why I Am Leaving Goldman Sachs," http://www.nytimes.com/2012/03/14/opinion/why-i-am-leaving-goldman-sachs.html.

10. http://www.fastcompany.com/1825404/cultures-big-business-moment.

11. http://www.google.com/about/company/facts/culture.

12. "Why I Left Google," http://blogs.msdn.com/b/jw_on_tech/archive/
    2012/03/13/why-i-left-google.aspx.

CHAPTER 6

1. http://techcrunch.com/2009/07/21/best-buy-goes-all-twitter-crazy
   -with-twelpforce/.
2. http://www.npr.org/blogs/thesalt/2011/10/26/141732915/customer
   -outrage-forces-necco-to-put-artificial-ingredients-back-into-wafers.
3. http://www.thecentsiblelife.com/2009/12/good-customer-service
   -trader-joes/.
4. http://www.fastcompany.com/magazine/87/customer-traderjoes
   .html.
5. http://adage.com/article/news/gap-scrap-logo-return-design/
   146417/.
6. http://techcrunch.com/2010/10/11/gap-logo-redesign/.
7. https://www.google.com/finance?client=ob&q=NYSE:GPS.
8. http://www.entrepreneur.com/article/223434.
9. http://www.nytimes.com/2012/03/01/education/digital-skills-can
   -be-quickly-acquired.html?pagewanted=all.

CHAPTER 7

1. http://articles.businessinsider.com/2011-04-13/tech/29957143_1_
   jack-dorsey-twitter-podcasting.
2. http://www.fastcompany.com/1834196/the-pivot.
3. http://www.businessweek.com/articles/2012-04-12/how-to-fail
   -mark-pincus.
4. http://finance.yahoo.com/q/ks?s=ZNGA.
5. http://blogs.barrons.com/techtraderdaily/2012/06/12/zynga-users
   -decline-as-more-facebook-usage-goes-mobile-says-cowen/.
6. http://blogs.wsj.com/deals/2012/06/15/sec-sought-increased-details
   -on-facebook-users-zynga/.
7. http://the99percent.com/articles/6211/The-McSweeneys-Mantra
   -Havent-Tried-It-Yet-Do-It-Anyway.
8. http://www.theatlantic.com/business/archive/2011/01/what-went
   -wrong-at-borders/69310/.
9. http://m.marketingprofs.com/charts/2011/6164/booz-adaptability-is
   -key-for-social-media-success.

CHAPTER 8

1. Jill Radsken, "Crunch 'n' Munch Guy Makes Spirited Career
   Change," *The Boston Herald*. December 19, 2002.
2. Richard C. Whiteley, *Love the Work You're With*, Henry Holt, 2001,
   p. 3.

3. Howard Schultz, *Onward: How Starbucks Fought for Its Life Without Losing Its Soul*, Rodale, 2011, p. iii.
4. http://www.evancarmichael.com/Famous-Entrepreneurs/3793/ Tuning-into-Tastes-The-Secret-of-Jones-Sodas-Success.html.
5. http://articles.marketwatch.com/2012-02-01/industries/ 31028974 _1_people-relationships-society.
6. http://www.businessinsider.com/facebook-movie-zuckerberg -ims?op=1.
7. http://news.byu.edu/archive11-mar-zuckerberg.aspx.
8. http://news.stanford.edu/news/2005/june15/jobs-061505.html.
9. http://blogs.wsj.com/middleseat/2009/03/16/southwests-rapping -flight-attendant-on-freestyle-and-flying-to-vegas.
10. Whiteley, *Love the Work You're With*, pp. 5, 40.
11. http://blogs.reuters.com/small-business/2011/08/31/do-you-want -to-sell-sugar-water-or-do-you-want-to-change-the-world.

CHAPTER 9

1. http://www.stanford.edu/group/knowledgebase/cgi-bin/2010/10/20/ hsieh-of-zappos-takes-happiness-seriously/.
2. http://aboutfoursquare.com/klm-surprise/.

CHAPTER 10

1. http://hbr.org/2012/05/to-keep-your-customers-keep-it-simple/ar/1.
2. Linda Tischler, "The Beauty of Simplicity," *Fast Company*, November 2005.
3. Ken Segall, *Insanely Simple*, Penguin, 2012, p. 149.
4. Ibid., p. 32.
5. http://www.crn.com/slide-shows/mobility/232500566/10-incredible -stats-from-apples-q1-earnings.htm?pgno=3.
6. Segall, *Insanely Simple*, p. 48.
7. Ibid., p. 51.
8. http://gizmodo.com/5878942/inside-instagram-how-slowing-its-roll -put-the-little-startup-in-the-fast-lane.
9. http://nymag.com/daily/intel/2012/04/facebook-and-instagram -when-your-favorite-app-sells-out.html.
10. http://www.msnbc.msn.com/id/46897956/ns/business-us_business/ t/blackberry-giving-consumer-market.

CHAPTER 11

1. http://www.toms.com/corporate-info.
2. http://online.wsj.com/article/SB100014240527487042439045756305 41486290052.html?KEYWORDS=Grateful+People+Are+Happier+ Healthier+Long+After.
3. http://blogs.hbr.org/cs/2010/12/is_gms_gratitude_worth_sharing .html.

Index

Dave Kerpen is the cofounder and CEO of Likeable, an award-winning social media and word-of-mouth marketing firm comprised of communications and consultancy agency Likeable Media, and software platform Likeable Local. Dave and his wife, Carrie, lead a team of more than 60 people in working with brands, organizations, governments, and small businesses to better leverage social media to become more  transparent, responsive, engaged, and likeable. Likeable was named to both the 2011 and 2012 Inc. 500 list of fastest-growing private companies in the United States.

Dave's first book, a *New York Times, USA Today,* and Amazon #1 bestseller, was *Likeable Social Media: How to Delight Your Customers, Create an Irresistible Brand, and Be Generally Amazing on Facebook (and Other Social Networks)*. His second book is titled *Likeable Business: Why Today's Consumers Demand More & How Leaders Can Deliver* (McGraw-Hill, November 2012).

Dave is a frequent keynote speaker at venues around the world and a contributing writer for Mashable, *Inc., Fast Company,* the Huffington Post, *Forbes,* and the *Washington Post.* His work has been featured on CNBC's *On the Money, ABC World News Tonight,* the *CBS Early Show, BBC World News,* and in the *New York Times,* among others.

Dave is proud of his Likeable business accomplishments but prouder of his other joint venture with Carrie: Charlotte and

Kate, their two daughters at home in Port Washington, New York.

dave@likeable.com
FB.com/DaveKerpen
@DaveKerpen

Theresa Braun graduated from Emerson College summa cum laude with a degree in marketing communication. She works as a marketing executive at Likeable. While she'll always be a Bostonian at heart, she's currently living in New York City.

theresa@likeable.com
FB.com/brauntm
@TheresaBraun

Valerie Pritchard is a public relations practitioner living in New York City. She graduated from Oklahoma State University and originally hails from Plano, Texas. This is her first contribution to a book, although her tweets and blog posts could probably be compiled into several.

Don't miss Dave Kerpen's *New York Times* and *USA Today* bestseller *Likeable Social Media!*

"Kerpen's insights and clear, how-to instructions on building brand popularity . . . are nothing short of brilliant."

—Jim McCann, founder of 1-800-FLOWERS.COM and Celebrations.com

FOR MORE ABOUT THE BOOK, visit LikeableBook.com.

TO LEARN MORE ABOUT THE AUTHOR, visit davekerpen.com.

Learn more. McGraw Hill Do more.
MHPROFESSIONAL.COM

WE ARE THE
PEOPLE
BEHIND YOUR NEXT
SOCIAL MEDIA
SUCCESS STORY

21x   MORE ENGAGING CONTENT

41%   FASTER RESPONSIVENESS ON FACEBOOK AND TWITTER

74%   CONVERSION RATE FOR FACEBOOK ADS

2x   OUR CLIENTS' FACEBOOK FANS SPEND 2X MORE THAN THEIR NON-FAN CUSTOMERS

To learn more about Likeable Media, including free resources and blog, please visit **likeable.com**.

To learn more about Dave as a speaker, please visit **davekerpen.com**.